"God Help the Irish!"

The History of the Irish Brigade

Phillip Thomas Tucker

McWhiney Foundation Press
McMurry University
Abilene, Texas

Library of Congress Cataloging-in-Publication Data

Tucker, Phillip Thomas, 1953-
God help the Irish!: the history of the Irish Brigade /
Phillip Thomas Tucker.
p. cm.
Includes bibliographical references and index.
ISBN-13: 978-1-893114-50-0 (pbk.: alk. paper)
ISBN-10: 1-893114-50-3 (pbk.: alk. paper)
1. United States. Army of the Potomac. Irish Brigade. 2. United States–
History–Civil War, 1861-1865–Participation, Irish American. 3. Irish
American soldiers–History–19th century. 4. United States. Army of the
Potomac. Irish Brigade–Biography. 5. Irish American soldiers–Biography.
6. United States–History–Civil War, 1861-1865–Regimental histories.
7. United States–History–Civil War, 1861-1865–Campaigns. I. Title.

E493.5.I683T83 2006
973.7'410899162–dc22

2006016121

McWhiney Foundation Press
McMurry Station, Box 637
Abilene, TX 79697-0637
(325) 572-3974
(325) 572-3991 fax
www.mcwhiney.org/press

Printed in the United States of America

Distributed by Texas A&M University Press Consortium
www.tamu.edu/upress
1-800-826-8911

ISBN-10: 1-893114-50-3
ISBN-13: 978-1-893114-50-0
10 9 8 7 6 5 4 3 2 1

Book Designed by Rosenbohm Graphic Design

DEDICATION

To my Irish ancestors, who fought on both sides
of the Mississippi.

TABLE OF CONTENTS

PHOTOGRAPHS AND ILLUSTRATIONS

All photographs and illustrations are from the
Library of Congress.

MAPS

All maps by Donald S. Frazier

INTRODUCTION

During the Civil War, nearly 150,000 Irish soldiers served in Union armies on both sides of the Mississippi River. The vast majority of these Irishmen fought as members of units that were made up mostly of native born Americans rather than immigrants. So many Irish had migrated to the northern United States during the Great Famine of the 1840s that even with the figure of nearly 150,000 soldiers, the number represents only a small percentage of the men that could have fought for the Union. The opposite situation was true in the South. Here, according to some estimates, as many as 30,000 Irish served in Confederate armies, a high percentage of the overall Irish male population. In a direct reversal of the immigrant Irish who served in Union armies, the Confederate Irishmen volunteered for service in large numbers.

This discrepancy can be explained by a number of distinct factors. For one, large numbers of the Irish in America in 1861 were staunch Democrats. Many Irish in America were unwilling to fight for the Union because they perceived the conflict as an aggressive war of invasion against an agrarian people of the South who, they felt, in many ways, resembled the rural Irish still in the old country. The bitter lessons of Great Britain's autocratic rule of Ireland caused many Irish to perceive the struggle in America as an unjust and immoral war of conquest to bring the wayward seceded states back into the Union by force. As a result, many Irish in America sympathized with the infant Confederacy and its plight. They saw the northern war effort as comparable to the centralized power and military might of a powerful Great Britain subjugating a culturallly distinct, agrarian people in a rural land—Ireland.

Religion was another factor that explained why so many Irishmen did not serve in the armies of the Union. These mainly Catholic immigrants and refugees of the Great Famine, viewed the North as a powerful Protestant majority forcing its will upon a minority. Many Irish viewed the situation in the United States in 1861 as analogous to Protestant England conquering and then ruling the Catholic people of Ireland for centuries.

Total numbers or percentages fail fully to explain the importance of the overall Irish contribution to the Union war effort, however. More important than actual numbers was the crucial timing of the Irish contribution to the Union war effort. Large numbers of Irishmen across the North continued to join Union armies, especially the Army of the Potomac, throughout the later course of the war even when enlistments overall decreased sharply. Especially in 1863-1865, many Americans across the North sought to avoid military service and evade the draft because of spiraling casualty rates in a lengthy war.

With the slaughter increasing on both sides, the manpower-short Confederacy eventually recognized that it was on the losing end of a war of attrition. Union armies were able to quickly refill their thinned ranks after each major battle, even though the war-weary northern populace was much less likely to volunteer for military service. The explanation was that the North replenished its ranks by recruiting the newly arrived immigrant Irish at the major port cities of the northeast, such as New York and Boston. Some especially enterprising Union recruiters were even active in Ireland. On the Emerald Isle they recruited men for service in Union armies at such principal port cities as Galway and Cork. This carefully calculated Union policy of targeting Irish immigrants for recruitment proved highly successful at a time when manpower was badly needed to fuel the drive towards victory. By the time Gen. Robert E. Lee and his battered Army of Northern Virginia were forced to surrender at Appomattox Court House, Virginia, on Palm Sunday 1865, an estimated one in three soldiers in the Army of the Potomac were of foreign birth—most significantly from Ireland. Clearly, during the later years of the conflict when the war was its most unpopular among the northern people, the steady flow of Irishmen into the ranks of the Army of the Potomac played a key role in ensuring ultimate victory.

The key timing—from 1863 to 1865—of this manpower contribution of the Irish to winning the decisive Union victory has been largely overlooked by historians. A wide range of factors can explain this negligence. One reason for this omission was that a single combat brigade overshadowed the overall role played by the Irish in the Union war effort. Consequently, one combat unit of the Army of the Potomac came to symbolize and represent the overall Irish contribution in the Civil War. This enduring legacy continues to garner recognition for this distinguished Irish combat unit to this day. Both then and now, the primary interest in the Irish effort in the Union Armies during the Civil War has been largely centered upon the most ethnically and culturally distinct brigade of the Army of the Potomac—the famed Irish Brigade.

But why was so much emphasis placed on the performance and role of the Irish Brigade during the war? Why was the role of the Irish Brigade so well-covered and publicized by northern journalists and writers during the war years? How did the reputation of a single unit of Irish soldiers of the Army of the Potomac grow so far out of proportion to the contributions of larger numbers of Irishmen in blue who served with distinction during the war years? To understand the Irish Brigade's pivotal role in such major battles as Antietam, Fredericksburg, and Gettysburg, it is important to attempt to ascertain what factors caused these men to become some of the finest combat troops of the Civil War.

The enduring fame of the Irish Brigade was the product, not only of its superior combat performances on the major battlefields of the eastern theater, but also of its distinctive ethnic qualities, Gaelic ways, and high sacrifice. As one of the elite combat units of the Civil War, the hard-fighting Irish Brigade became as much a part of legend as of fact in the national consciousness.

The relatively low participation of the Irish in Union armies in relation to their overall numbers in the North occurred in part because the recent arrivals from Ireland, who were mostly Catholics, found that a hostile Protestant America and an impoverished status awaited them in the new world. Nevertheless, this unfavorable social and eco-

Veteran officers of the Irish Brigade

nomic situation helped to set the motivational stage for the soldiers of the Irish Brigade who wanted to demonstrate their equality and worth—to excel on the battlefield while in the spotlight of a national audience. Northern newspapers and people focused so much attention on the performance of this lone Irish unit largely because the North was yet skeptical of the loyalty, character, and courage of the Irish soldier. Quite simply, at the war's beginning, non-Irish Northerners believed that the Irish were vastly inferior soldiers. Much of the North's focus on the Irish Brigade was initially to trumpet its anticipated failure, which would in turn support the widespread anti-Irish, anti-Catholic, and anti-immigrant views of many northern Protestants.

Even in the midst of war, many Northerners questioned the quality of the Irish character, especially that of the Irish Catholics. Negative stereotypes perpetuated by anti-Irish, anti-Catholic, and anti-immigrant Americans still held sway in the minds of some Northerners. Many feared that the Irish were more loyal to the Pope and Catholicism than their adopted homeland, and others wondered if the Emerald Islanders would serve with honor while fighting in behalf of a largely Protestant nation.

The young officers and men of the Irish Brigade attempted to answer these allegations with their battlefield performance. The soldiers, especially leading officers, deliberately cultivated and coveted publicity to highlight their contributions and sacrifices for the Union. Irish Brigade troops were determined that their superior battlefield performances would provide a shining representative example of the heroism of the Irish fighting man for all America to see. Both the strength of anti-Irish feelings and the harsh realities of life for the immigrant Irish in America ensured that the Irish Brigade troops were highly motivated and determined to succeed at all costs. They wanted to demonstrate once and for all, to a skeptical America, that they could serve as honorably and fight as well as the average American citizen, showing that the Irish people deserved equality in American society.

Across the North, tens of thousands of Irishmen served in approximately forty smaller-than-brigade-level units which consisted mostly or partially of Irish soldiers. But only one full brigade of all Irish warriors served in the Union forces. This infantry unit, the Irish Brigade, was known simply as "Meagher's Brigade," named in honor of its first commander, Thomas Francis Meagher. The Irish Brigade was one of the most colorful and culturally distinctive units of the Civil War. On the principal battlefields of the eastern theater, the Irish Brigade proved to be not only culturally unique, but also an elite combat unit.

During the war years, the reputation of the Irish Brigade grew to lofty heights. Since the attention of the eastern press and the northern people focused on the campaigns of the principal army in the eastern theater, the Army of the Potomac, the Irish Brigade received much notice.

Union Gen. Thomas Francis Meagher, the first commander of the Irish Brigade.

During some of the most important battles of the war, the Irish Brigade established a hard-earned and well-deserved reputation as a lethal fighting machine and one of the premier combat units of the Civil War. The Irish Brigade was often relied upon by top army, corps, and division commanders to spearhead an attack or to protect the army's withdrawal. In addition, the Irish Brigade won a reputation for performing complex and precise tactical maneuvers under heavy fire and during the most trying battlefield situations. As demonstrated repeatedly on the field of strife, the Irish Brigade's accomplishments and sacrifices either equaled or exceeded the battlefield performances of the best combat brigades not only of the Army of the Potomac, but of other Federal units as well. The cost in establishing this lofty reputation was frightfully high. More than 4,000 soldiers of the Irish Brigade were killed or wounded in the war. This devastating total loss was greater than the overall strength of the Irish Brigade at any one time during the war years.

Across the North, the widespread recognition of the Irish Brigade rose to such heights also because of the leading role the average infantry brigade played in Civil War armies. An infantry brigade usually consisted of around 2,000-2,500 men, and served as the central element of Civil War armies. With the capability to act tactically both on the march and on the battlefield as an autonomous unit within an overall flexible divisional structure, a single combat brigade, especially of an elite quality like the Irish Brigade, possessed sufficient strength, flexibility, and striking power to turn the tide of battle in a crisis situation.

The average infantry brigade during the Civil War was a microcosm of the society and community from which it was drawn. This was a central ingredient that made the Irish Brigade more distinctive and unique than any other brigade, Union or Confederate. While other brigades reflected the society of their region and state, the Irish Brigade, consisting of mostly Irish Catholic immigrants but some second generation Irishmen as well, reflected not only the immigrant society of America, but also the culture, pride, and heritage of an ancient Celtic land on the other side of the Atlantic. Even though most Irish Brigade soldiers were residents of New York City, Boston, and Philadelphia, these men were less influenced by their adopted American homeland than by the beliefs, value systems, and aspirations of the people of the Emerald Isle. Additionally, the Irish Brigade troops also mirrored the political and social values, cultural priorities, and nationalist sentiments of the immigrant Irish of the northeast United States.

The religious composition and the strong religious faith of its members also made the Irish Brigade distinctive. Most of the soldiers who were recent immigrants were Catholic and many of the second generation Irishmen were Catholic as well, though a few were Protestant. The Irish Brigade was the most Catholic unit of the Army of the Potomac, and this religious core fueled unit cohesion.

The aggressive manner in which the Irish Brigade troops fought on the battlefields of the eastern theater partly reflected a distinctive cultural tradition of Gaelic and Celtic warfare stemming from ancient times. The central quality of ancient Celtic tactics through centuries of warfare was a bold and aggressive type of fighting characterized most of all by the frontal attack. The recklessness, abandon, and courage of Celtic warriors became legendary in the annals of both ancient and recent European warfare. These unique Celtic qualities in traditional warfare were faithfully continued by the Irish Brigade soldiers on such bloody fields as Antietam, Fredericksburg, and Gettysburg.

Father William Corby, the chaplain of the Eighty-eighth New York, possessed a thorough knowledge of the tragic course of Irish history. He stated "[the Irish Brigade] springs from a fearless race, whose valor has been tested in a war that was incessant for three hundred years, with the Danes and Normans, followed by contests, more or less fierce, for centuries, with England." These distinctive Celtic qualities that had developed during centuries of warfare help to explain in part why the Irish Brigade became one of the premier combat brigades of the Civil War. Such factors also help explain why these Celtic warriors in blue became famous for their superior fighting qualities and tenacity on the battlefield, especially in leading frontal attacks.

The Irish Brigade soldiers, who had witnessed the horrors of Ireland's Great Potato Famine of the 1840s, blamed the British government for what they saw as a deliberate genocide program that resulted in thousands of Irish deaths. British mismanagement generated a keener political and social awareness among the Irish of the Great Famine and Civil War generation. This experience served as a key factor that promoted fiery nationalist leaders of Ireland, like Thomas Francis Meagher, to attempt to spark the Irish revolt of 1848. The Young Ireland Revolt of 1848 was the most influential revolutionary experience for the Irish of the Civil War generation.

By fighting against the Confederacy, the Irish Brigade soldiers saw themselves as striking a blow against the ever-growing power and prestige of Great Britain. To the average Irishman, Great Britain represented monarchy, oppression, and injustice. The English likely wanted an opportunity to recognize the Confederacy. If the South could win a decisive victory early in the conflict, it would divide the prosperous United States in half. In this way, Great Britain would be able to greatly diminish the power of its principal economic rival, while reaping a measure of revenge for losing the thirteen colonies during the American Revolution.

While the vast majority of Union soldiers fought only to defeat the Confederacy and save the Union, the Irish Brigade soldiers were deeply influenced by the historical legacy of Ireland that was far different from America's story. Whereas the United States symbolized hope, freedom, and the best prospects for the future, the tragic history of Ireland and the Irish experience represented the opposite: hundreds of years of frustration, oppression, and shattered dreams.

In a 1863 letter, Color Sgt. Peter Welsh, Twenty-eighth Massachusetts Volunteer Infantry, summarized the feeling of the Irish Brigade's soldiers in regard to what was a two-front war for the Irish in blue: "When we are fighting for America we are fighting in the interest of Irland [*sic*] striking a double blow cutting with a two edged sword[.] For while we strike in defence [*sic*] of the rights of Irishmen here we are striking a blow at Irlands [*sic*] enemy and oppressor England [which] hates this country because of its growing power and greatness [and] for its republican liberty. . . ."

The most visible example of the persistent loyalty to the great Irish dream of liberating Ireland from British domination among both the immigrant and second generation soldiers of the Irish Brigade could be found on their distinctive battle-flags. These silk battle-flags of emerald green, decorated with ancient Gaelic symbolism, flew with pride over the charging ranks of the Irish Brigade. Representing a revolutionary quest for Ireland's freedom, such green banners, that symbolized Irish nationalism, had flown proudly over rebellious armies of Irish Rebels in their doomed revolutionary struggles against the English.

The personification of this persistant sense of a vibrant
Irish nationalism was the unit's first and most inspirational
leader, Thomas Francis Meagher. Ironically, he was a diehard
Democrat, who felt great sympathy for the plight and nationalist aspirations of the South and its struggle for self-deter-
mination against a powerful centralized government.
Beloved by the Irish community of New York City and Irish
Brigade members for his activities as an Irish revolutionary
leader of the Young Ireland Movement of 1848, Meagher was
born to a wealthy merchant father who was mayor of the city
of Waterford on August 3, 1823. Meagher learned the value
of education and discipline at the strict environment of the
Jesuit colleges of Clongowes and Stonyhurst. Here, the
Jesuit priests helped to bestow upon the young man not only
a fine education, but also a strong Catholic faith. During
these formative years, Meagher also gained a greater sense
of Irish nationalism and he longed for Ireland's independence
from Great Britain. Meagher also felt the hope that the Irish
people would gain religious, economic, and social equalities
from the examples bestowed by the American and French
Revolutions. Meagher's maturing political and social awareness, fueled by a visit to revolutionary France, only further
created an Irish patriot and revolutionary.

Thereafter, Meagher dedicated his life toward the goal of
Ireland's liberation. Breaking away from the Irish moderates
and conservatives, Meagher became a fiery Irish radical. He
was an early vocal advocate of violent revolution as the solu-
tion for achieving Irish independence. Earning him the nickname "Meagher of the Sword," he espoused the use of the
sword, the implement of war for ancient Gaelic warriors, "as

a sacred weapon [which could take] the shape of the serpent and reddened the shroud of the oppressor with too deep a dye. . . ." Meagher believed that Ireland's freedom could only be achieved by way of a violent revolution. For Meagher, the idealistic goal of a free Ireland was well worth the cost, even if it meant sacrificing his own life.

Following the example of Robert Emmet's 1803 revolt and in the aftermath of the Great Potato Famine, Meagher became one of the principal leaders of yet another bid for Ireland's independence, and he placed all his hopes and efforts on the success of the "Young Ireland" revolt in 1848. Meagher explained the all-consuming passion of his life: "To lift this island up, to restore her native powers and her ancient constitution—this has been my ambition. . . ." Like other fiery Irish nationalists, Meagher viewed British domination as the great destroyer of Irish culture, Celtic-Gaelic society, and the Catholic faith. The dream of Meagher and other Young Irelanders of 1848 was "to sweep this island clear of British butchers and plant the green flag on Dublin Castle," for centuries the historic center of English power in Ireland. Along with other nationalist leaders, Meagher scoured the Irish countryside in an attempt to spark a grassroots revolt in the summer of 1848. The time was not yet ripe for revolution, and the budding revolutionary activities were brutally crushed by the British.

No widespread nationalist uprising occurred and Meagher was taken into custody. Meagher was thrown into the infamous Kilmainham Prison. Here, the young revolutionary Robert Emmet had spent his last night before his public execution in Dublin in September 1803. Despite the failure of the Young Ireland revolt, Meagher gained more popularity among the Irish people when imprisoned. While in British hands, he gave an impassioned speech during a show trial that was well-publicized. Meagher's memorable speech "scarcely ranks second to Robert Emmet's death speech," wrote fellow nationalist David Power Conyngham.

Narrowly escaping execution, Meagher and several other Young Ireland leaders were banished for life to the island of Tasmania. But the penal colony off the coast of Australia could not contain the ambitions of the exiled Meagher. Thanks to the assistance of an old Irish Rebel who had been banished for his role in the 1798 Revolution, Meagher escaped to the United States in 1852 to become a free man once again. Fleeing to the large Irish community of New York City, Meagher started a new life, like so many other of his exiled countrymen.

Meagher became a hero of the Irish community not only in New York, but also across the United States. His revolutionary fame and reputation preceded him. Meagher was especially well-known in Ireland and the United States for his eloquent defense during his Dublin trial: ". . . the history of Ireland explains my crime and justifies it [and] judged by that history, the treason of which I have been convicted loses all guilt—is sanctified as a duty—will be ennobled as a sacrifice."

A widower after his first wife's death, Meagher married the daughter of another Irish exile, who was now a wealthy merchant of New York City. Meagher enhanced his already lofty reputation among the Irish community of New York City by gaining more renown as an orator, lawyer, scholar, and

Lyrics to the song "Meagher is Leading the Irish Brigade."

editor of an Irish-American newspaper. Meagher also possessed an adventurous side and remained a revolutionary at heart, even engaging in American filibuster activities in Central America. When the war erupted in April 1861, the eyes of the Irish community naturally turned to their dynamic revolutionary hero.

A powerful nationalist motivation and spirit remained alive and well among many Irish Brigade soldiers. These Irishmen in blue were inspired by Meagher's words, motivating the Irish soldiers to achieve battlefield successes to pave the way for political and social gains for the Irish people in America. Meagher often reminded his Irish Brigade soldiers during the war years, "today to preserve America, tomorrow to liberate Ireland."

For many Irish Brigade soldiers, fighting to save the Union was much about struggling for the betterment of future generations of the Irish people in America. In a winter 1863 letter, Color Sgt. Peter Welsh summarized one of the primary reasons why the Irish Brigade soldiers fought to save "this republic [which] as it grew in strenght [sic] its influence has compelled her to grant more liberal laws and in other nations it had the same efect [sic] but if it should now fall then away with all hope of liberty in europe and particularly in poor old Erin." For some soldiers of the Irish Brigade, saving the Union ensured that America would continue to serve as a shining beacon of hope and a refuge for future generations of Irish immigrants. Indeed, the high motivation of the Irish Brigade soldiers was described by the words of Gen. James Shields, a native of County Tyrone in northern Ireland. He emphasized the nature of their unique struggle while addressing the Irish Brigade soldiers: "You fight in a sacred cause[.] Two worlds are watching you."

Bound together by a sense of both Irish and American patriotism, Irishmen primarily from three major northeastern cities—New York City, Philadelphia, and Boston—merged together in common purpose. This mingling of Irishmen from different areas across the North embodied an acclimation process that was quite unlike the experience of soldiers in an average infantry brigade of the Civil War. While the average infantry brigade usually represented rural areas and small towns or a single large city, such units almost never hailed primarily from a trio of major cities like the Irish Brigade.

Even class differences were overcome for common purpose when the Irish Brigade formed. The lower class Irish elements of common laborers, canal diggers, railroad workers, and other menial occupations united with solidly middle class Irishmen and even lower upper class Irishmen, who were successful merchants, teachers, and lawyers in New York City, Boston, and Philadelphia. The birth of the Irish Brigade bound these different classes into one body of united soldiery.

Now the Irish soldiers in blue, from lowly tenant farmer to successful attorney, shared common interests and mutual goals in battling to save the Union. While the immigrant Irish represented the lower or poor class, the leading officers at the brigade, regimental, and even company level, were more often second generation Irish and established members of society. In the United States, the lower class Irish endured little more than a hand-to-mouth existence in the dismal

Irish ghettos and filthy boarding houses of the major northeast cities, living in squalid conditions that mocked the American dream. The middle class Irish, who migrated from mostly the towns and cities of Ireland, usually retained their middle class status in America thanks primarily to relatively higher levels of education and income.

These combined political, social, and nationalist goals and dreams, that stemmed from both the distinctive Irish and American experiences, produced perhaps the most highly motivated, disciplined, and determined soldiery of the Civil War. These distinctive factors played key roles in transforming the Irish Brigade into an elite unit, one of the best combat units of the Army of the Potomac.

Lt. Richard Turner, who served on General Meagher's staff, wrote of the magical effect of the sudden appearance of the cheering Irish Brigade troops on other Union soldiers in the heat of battle, especially those who had wavered at the decisive moment: "I pledge you my word that when the Irish Brigade approaches the turning point of the battles, the hearts of that portion of the army that see them are moved within them, the most graceful and glad cheers greet us all the way, the wounded take heart, and the beaten and broken, reassured, join in our sturdy ranks and go along with renewed courage to the front line.—That is the Irish Brigade." This widespread psychological affect of the mere sight of the Irish Brigade in lifting the morale of Union troops was especially beneficial to the battered Army of the Potomac during some of its most severe battlefield challenges.

By examining the Irish Brigade not only by its tactical prowess on the battlefield but also by its composition, demographics, and demeanor, a larger and clearer picture of the unit and its importance to the Army of the Potomac and the northern American-Irish population can be gleaned.

Phillip Thomas Tucker
Washington, D.C.

CHAPTER 1

The Call to Arms

It was only natural that the Irish of New York City rallied around Thomas Francis Meagher in the first year of the Civil War. After the 1848 Young Ireland Revolt, Meagher became the most visible symbolic figure for Irish nationalism, and a prominent Irish-American leader once he immigrated to the United States.

In Arlington, Virginia, just west of Washington, D.C., the North unleashed its first major offensive of the war, calculated to eventually capture Richmond, Virginia, and win the war in one stroke. Commanding the overly-confident Union Army, Gen. Irvin McDowell advanced upon the Confederate army positioned around the key railroad junction at Manassas, Virginia. Here, the Union Army was beaten by the southern force under Gen. Pierre Gustave Toutant Beauregard on July 21, 1861, amid the parched fields overlooking a small muddy stream called Bull Run. It was not only the first major defeat of the North, but also the first rout of the principal Union army in the east.

Officers of the 69th New York at Fort Corcoran a week before First Bull Run.

As the shattered remains of the vanquished army fled for the safety of the nation's capital after ten hours of combat, one of the few Federal units that stood firm amid the chaos was a feisty infantry regiment of Irish soldiers. This unit was the Sixty-ninth New York State Militia, the most famous militia unit in the United States. The Sixty-ninth New York State Militia consisted of well-trained men, mostly Catholics from New York City. These militiamen could trace their unit's proud lineage back to an earlier period when the volunteers had worn uniforms of green in honor of old Ireland. In the midst of the first Union disaster of the war, the prewar discipline and training of the Sixty-ninth New York rose to the fore.

The Irish soldiers of the Sixty-ninth New York had joined the escalating battle earlier in the day as part of the Union attack that surged up Matthew's Hill. The fighting ebbed and flowed until the Federal troops captured the key high ground. The Union assault continued up the slope of the Henry House Hill, just south of Matthew's Hill. Where other Yankee units had failed to carry the elevated position, the Irish captured the high ground in a slashing attack that one Irish soldier said demonstrated "all the impetuosity of our race. . . ." Counterattacking Confederates eventually carried the field, hurling the Yankee units rearward and off the heights of Chinn Ridge and Henry Hill in the late afternoon. The day was won for the Confederacy.

During the confused retreat of the Union Army from the Bull Run battlefield, the Sixty-ninth New York State Militia was one of the few units of the Union Army that maintained its discipline and cohesion in the rout. Although the term of enlistment for the volunteer unit had expired, the soldiers had voted to continue active service. To withstand the Confederate pursuit with a bold front, these well-trained Irishman formed a classic Napoleonic hollow square that was effective in repelling cavalry. All the while, the unit's green battle-flag representing their Irish heritage waved above the formation of troops.

In the role of rear guard, the group of Irish troops helped to slow the tide of Confederate progress as General Beauregard ordered a general advance to exploit the tactical advantage. For their steadfast actions during the retreat from Bull Run, these tough New Yorkers won a well-deserved reputation across the North as the "Fighting Irish." Amid the

A picture of the Matthew's house, north of Henry House, after the battle of Bull Run.

defeat at First Bull Run, these Celtic troops became among the first war heroes of the North.

One Irish officer who performed with distinction during the disaster at First Bull Run was the commander of a company of red-uniformed soldiers known as the Irish Zouaves, Company F, Sixty-ninth New York State Militia— Capt. Thomas Francis Meagher. The dashing Captain Meagher gained widespread recognition for the inspiring leadership he displayed at First Bull Run. To encourage his men to hold firm against the victorious rebels, Meagher waved his saber and yelled to his Irishmen:

Judith Henry's house after the battle of Bull Run.

"Boys! Look at that [emerald green] flag—remember Ireland and Fontenoy!"

Even when the Sixty-ninth New York started to lose its cohesion after the fall of nearly 200 men, Meagher and his disciplined Irish Zouaves of Company K remained firmly in position. These soldiers were among the last organized groups of Federal troops to depart the disastrous field of Bull Run. With leading officers either shot down or captured, Captain Meagher, now the acting major of the regiment, demonstrated his leadership by bearing the green flag him-

*A drawing by an Irish Brigade soldier of "the plains of Manassas"
from Meagher's Headquarters.*

self to inspire his Company K soldiers to stand firm. Near the end of the action, Meagher was knocked unconscious when his horse was shot from under him. Fortunately, he was carried to safety before the Confederates took over the position.

On the ill-fated field of Bull Run, Captain Meagher enhanced his already lofty reputation. The spirited role of the "Fighting Irish" was one of the few bright highlights of the Union defeat. The battle was not an ending, but a beginning of sorts for Meagher. He envisioned a leading role for himself and the Irish soldiers that went far beyond leading a single company into combat.

In the aftermath of the Union fiasco at First Bull Run, civilian and military leaders across the North searched for explanations to understand the defeat. Northern leadership

sought to ascertain solutions in order to avoid future rever-
sals. Inspired by the performance of the "Fighting Irish,"
Meagher began to conceive the idea of forming an entire
brigade of Irishmen to serve in the principal Union army in
the eastern theater. The former Young Irelander was con-
vinced that the legendary fighting spirit and superior battlefield capabilities of the Irish soldier could make an impact in
the war, and hasten decisive victory for the unprepared
North.

The idealistic Meagher envisioned the formation of an
entire brigade composed of Irishmen and led by Irish officers. This was a unique concept in America, but not an original one in the history of armies around the world. The
annals of European military history offered a number of
examples of Irish Brigades that served European monarchs
with distinction. No single historical example of the role
played by an Irish Brigade lingered more in the minds of
Meagher and his men than the performance at the battle of
Fontenoy, Belgium. To repeat the glories of Fontenoy and
other European battlefields, Meagher planned to reconstruct
the elite, highly-disciplined Irish Brigade. This new unit
would consist of a number of Irish infantry regiments that
would be trained to duplicate the heroic feats of the famed
Irish Brigade of old. Meagher hoped to recapture the pride
and spirit of Fontenoy in the new Irish Brigade of the Army
of the Potomac.

Fontenoy was no idle inspiration for the Irishmen of the
Civil War generation. By the time of the Civil War, few chap-
ters of Irish military history were more celebrated than the
performance of an Irish brigade at the battle of Fontenoy in

1745. During the conflict known as King George's War, a French army under Gen. Maurice Comte de Saxe met the British and their allies at the village of Fontenoy. Striking first, the British took the offensive, assailing the defensive position held by the French army, which included an Irish Brigade. The British troops were on the verge of winning the day when the Irishmen were ordered to launch a bayonet attack in hopes of turning the tide of battle.

Six regiments of Irish troops under Charles O'Brien struck the right of the advancing English line and hurled the British rearward. The Irish Brigade delivered the decisive blow that resulted in victory for the combined French and Dutch army. The Irish troops fought magnificently, charging forward with abandon, while unleashing the spirited Gaelic war cry, "Remember Limerick and Saxon treachery!" This yell was a reference to the legendary defiance of the Irish rebels of Limerick, a town besieged by forces under Prince William of Orange. The episode ended with Limerick's surrender and the signing of the Treaty of Limerick in 1691. Protestant rule in Ireland strengthened thereafter when this treaty was violated with the imposition of the infamous Penal Laws that stripped the Irish Catholics of their land, culture, and religion.

The role of the old Irish Brigade at the battle of Fontenoy additionally garnered a reputation for the Irish as the elite troops of all Europe, and Meagher was determined that the soldiers of the new Irish Brigade would win a comparable reputation as the best fighters in America. The slogan "Remember Fontenoy!," became as meaningful and inspirational battle-cry as "Remember the Alamo" did for Texans or the name of Bunker Hill to Americans of the pre-Civil War

generation. Not surprisingly, recruiting posters in New York
City utilized these historical mottos and others: "Irishmen,
you are training to meet your English enemies," and
"Remember Fontenoy!" Meagher often reminded the Irishmen
that the United States was now under a threat as serious as
England's conquest of Ireland.

Motivated by such emotional appeals, hundreds of Irish
volunteers of New York City poured forth to enlist in the Irish
Brigade for a period of three years. Meagher also gained support from New York's Archbishop John Hughes, who encouraged members of his flock to enlist in the Irish Brigade.
Rushing to the ranks were men born on the Emerald Isle and
second generation Irish born in the United States. Some soldiers were born in Canada, where they or their ancestors had
migrated from Ireland before pushing farther south to make
a new life for themselves in the United States.

Irish volunteers came from across the North. Capt. David
Power Conyngham, who served on Meagher's staff, noted
that, "So great was the rush of Irishmen to the ranks of the
Brigade, that recruits came from Albany, Utica, Buffalo,
Pittsburgh, and other remote towns and places." Some Irish
volunteers hailed from Chicago, Illinois. These were members of the Col. James A. Mulligan's Irish unit, the Twenty-
third Illinois Volunteer Infantry, which had been captured by
Gen. Sterling Price's Missouri State Guard troops at the battle of Lexington, Missouri, in late September 1861. After
these Irishmen were exchanged, they enlisted in Company D,
Sixty-ninth New York Volunteer Infantry.

While most New Yorkers joining the Irish Brigade hailed
from the city of New York and Manhattan Island, a good many

Col. James A. Mulligan, commander of the Twenty-third Illinois Volunteer Infantry.

other volunteers came from the surrounding areas, particularly Brooklyn and the New Jersey shore. The veterans of the Sixty-ninth New York State Militia served as an experienced nucleus for the fast-forming Irish Brigade. In total, around 500 members of the old Sixty-ninth flocked to the ranks of three newly formed New York regiments: the Sixty-third, Sixty-ninth, and the Eighty-eighth New York Volunteer Infantry. These regiments became the central core of the Irish Brigade.

The first regiment to fill its ranks with zealous young volunteers was the Sixty-ninth New York. Organized at Fort Schuyler, the regiment contained the majority of the former members of the militia regiment of the same name. The Sixty-ninth New York Volunteer Infantry was presented its colors in the home of Archbishop John Hughes on November 18, 1861. The formation of the Sixty-ninth New York was followed by the Eighty-eighth New York Volunteer Infantry, also organized at Fort Schuyler. With each passing day, Meagher's dream of creating an Irish Brigade was coming into reality. During the same ceremony at Archbishop Hughes's residence on Madison Avenue, the Eighty-eighth New York was presented its battle-flag by General Meagher's wife. The bond forged by this solemn presentation of the flag and other patriotic acts earned the regiment the nickname of "Mrs. Meagher's Own." The Sixty-third New York Volunteer Infantry formed soon afterwards at Camp Karrigan on

Col. James D. Brady (seated at right), commander of the 63rd New York pictured with Irish Brigade flag.

Staten Island, completing the filling of the Irish Brigade's ranks. Meagher's vision and appeal resulted in the formation of the first and only all-Irish brigade, consisting of more than 2,500 soldiers in blue.

The Irish Brigade was officially established on September 4, 1861. Meagher was determined that the unit become an elite military organization of the finest order. Consequently, much training and discipline was instilled upon the new soldiers of the Irish Brigade during the winter of 1861-1862. In many ways, the spirit and memory of the glories of Fontenoy and other European battlefields was being resurrected on American soil.

The ranks of the newly formed Irish Brigade contained a good percentage of veterans of the United States Army. These ex-regulars had fought from the swamps and hammocks of Florida during the Seminole Wars to the conquest of Mexico City during the Mexican-American War. Some volunteers had served in various European armies including Irish regiments of the British army, and in the Papal Army of Pius IX. Other Irish Brigade members had battled in behalf of the Republic of Mexico alongside their fellow Catholics. Lt. George Halpin, 116th Pennsylvania, had served in the British Army, campaigning in the jungles and mountains of India.

Reliable veterans such as Capt. Patrick Felan Clooney were scattered thickly throughout the Irish Brigade's ranks. At age twenty-one, Clooney led Company E, Eighty-eighth New York. Like many other Irish Brigade soldiers, Clooney had already acquired considerable military experience by the time of the Civil War's beginning. Before Clooney was recognized for valor at First Bull Run as a member of the Sixty-ninth New York State Militia, he had fought with the St. Patrick's Battalion of the Papal Brigade in the defense of Pope IX and the Papal city of Rome, Italy. The Irish Battalion of St. Patrick defended the Papal States around Rome in 1860 when an invading Italian army sought to destroy the power of the Catholic Church and to unify Italy through conquest. Clooney and around 1,400 other Irish had volunteered to defend the Pope and the Papal States in a crusade to save Roman Catholicism. Clooney survived a number of bloody battles in Italy, and returned home to Ireland with the survivors of the Irish Battalion of St. Patrick, just in time to learn the exciting news that the Young Irelander, Thomas F. Meagher, was forming a new Irish Brigade. Clooney departed immediately for America, embarking upon his next challenge.

Other veterans of the St. Patrick's Battalion who served in Italy were sprinkled throughout the Irish Brigade's ranks. Capt. John Dillion Mulhall of Boyle in western Ireland was known for his "restless spirit" throughout the Sixty-ninth New York. Mulhall was especially proud of his service as an officer of the St. Patrick's Battalion. He often showed other brigade members his Medal of St. Peter, Order of St. Sebastian, and other decorations he had earned fighting in the mountains of Italy for Roman Catholicism.

Another savvy veteran of the Papal Brigade was Capt. John H. Gleeson, Sixty-third New York. A native of County Tipperary in south central Ireland who migrated to America in 1861, Gleeson was destined to become the colonel of the Sixty-third New York by the war's end. The veterans of the St. Patrick Battalion who disembarked at the port of Cork, Ireland, amid an enthusiastic reception by the people of County Cork possessed plenty of combat experience. As important to them, these veterans embraced the memories of having served a holy cause in behalf of Pope Pius IX and Catholicism.

Other Irish Brigade troops possessed ample fighting experience as well. Dublin-born Lt. John T. Kavanaugh, Company I, Sixty-third New York, played a leading role in setting the stage for the largest clash of arms during the abortive revolt of 1848. Kavanaugh fled to America after the episode to start a new life. The exiled Irish revolutionary was later joined by his family.

Another Young Ireland revolutionary in the Irish Brigade was the ever-popular Capt. James E. McGee. He was a newspaper editor in both Ireland and the United States.

Once the war started and the Irish Brigade was formed, he served as the commander of the regimental color company, Company F, of the Sixty-ninth New York. McGee had been an official in one of the Confederate Clubs of Dublin during the Young Ireland Movement of 1848. After the Young Ireland Movement failed, he was forced to migrate to America.

Even some of the medical men of the Irish Brigade possessed distinguished revolutionary backgrounds in part because they were members of the educated and politically-enlightened middle class of Ireland. Laurence Reynolds of the Sixty-third New York was born in Meagher's hometown of Waterford. Reynolds proved to be an excellent surgeon, "although advanced in years [but] young in vigor." Refined and well-educated, the dedicated Irish surgeon was among "those of his countrymen who had to fly from Ireland in '48, his only crime being that he loved his country dearly." He was a romantic and notable poet, who was known as the "Poet Laureate" of the Irish Brigade. Reynolds' poems about the haunting beauty of Ireland and its romantic history were popular throughout the Irish Brigade.

The surgeon's brother, Francis Reynolds, served as the surgeon of the Eighty-eighth New York. Good-natured and jovial, Francis Reynolds had gained invaluable medical experience as an army surgeon in British service during the Crimean War. This experience helped to ensure that "he had no superior in the Army of the Potomac, particularly in operative surgery."

One capable assistant surgeon of the Irish Brigade, Dr. James Purcell of County Tipperary, Ireland, was the son of an Irish revolutionary of 1848. For these revolutionary exiles, service in the Irish Brigade now offered a new beginning and a renewal of old nationalist dreams.

Capt. David Power Conyngham, the son of tenant farmers from County Tipperary, Ireland, was a regional leader in the Young Ireland Movement. A scholarly intellectual, the handsome young Irishman served as an esteemed member of General Meagher's staff.

Another Young Irelander in the ranks of the Irish Brigade was Capt. William Horgan. He was described as "a gallant and distinguished officer," who first won distinction during the Peninsula Campaign. He had risen to the rank of major of the Eighty-eighth New York by the time he was killed at the battle of Fredericksburg.

Capt. David Power Conyngham, a member of Gen. Thomas Francis Meagher's staff.

These diehard Irish nationalists, General Meagher, Captain McGee, Major Horgan, Captain Conyngham, and Lieutenant Kavanaugh, were inspirational leaders of the Irish Brigade. They had dedicated their lives to freeing Ireland from British rule, only to be exiled for their politics. Many idealistic young soldiers of the Irish Brigade yet dreamed about liberating Ireland after gaining sufficient military experience in this struggle against the Confederacy. Not surprisingly, the Irish Brigade served as a center of Fenian agitation. The Fenians of the Irish Brigade formed the "Officer's Circle" of the Fenian Brotherhood. This organization, dedicated to the violent overthrow of British rule in Ireland, was also known as the "Fenian Circle of the Army of the Potomac." Surgeon Reynolds of the Sixty-third New York played a leading role in the organization's activities. One Irish Brigade member explained that the unit consisted of "high-souled, high-toned young Irish patriots, who had imbibed from his lips their passionate love of Ireland, and the hope in which they died, that some day or another they would have an opportunity to draw their swords . . . and display their soldierly skill to some purpose, in the ranks of men fighting for the Fatherland."

The Irish Brigade consisted of a supremely committed group of men. A second generation Irishman of the Eighty-eighth New York described the overall high quality of the Irish Brigade troops, who were "healthy, intelligent men, far above the average, and in many cases of liberal education . . . In my own regiment, as private soldiers, there were seven first-class lawyers!" The promising young Irishmen of Meagher's staff, such as Lt. Temple Emmet and Capt. John J. Gosson, were described as appearing like a group of festive "fox hunters [and] a class of Irish exquisites . . . good for a fight, card party or a hurdle jumping." Gosson had served in the Austrian army in a cavalry regiment.

The fighting spirit of these Irish soldiers was exceptionally high. Even before his first battle, Lt. Bernard S. O'Neill wrote to his mother that he and his comrades in Company C, Sixty-ninth New York, were especially eager "to have a forward agressive [sic] movement [in order] to bring our green colours through its Baptism of Blood." Young O'Neill had first heard of the Irish Brigade's formation when living a comfortable life in Ireland. "In the summer of 1861 when this Rebellion broke out," he wrote, "I was in the Old Country, when the news reached there of the President's proclamation for 500,000 troops[.] I immediately threw up a lucrative position, sailed from Ireland on the 7th Sept. arrived in New York and enlisted in the Irish Brigade without bounty or any other inducement on the 23 Sept. 1861."

The zealous Irishmen continued the process of becoming soldiers with a vigorous regime of training and drill. Officers worked long and hard to transform civilians into soldiers on the parade ground of Fort Schuyler on Long Island. Time was of the essence; indeed, there was relatively little time for the complete transformation of these Irishmen into well-trained and disciplined soldiers. The Emerald Islanders proved highly motivated, however, which compensated in part for the lack of thorough training.

The first challenge for the newly formed Irish Brigade was not long in coming. These "exiles of Erin from Munster's sunny plains, from Connaught's heights, and Leinster's vales" were about to enter the vortex of the storm. Many Irish Brigade soldiers, non-veterans and young men, were naive about the ways of war. As if believing that they were about to engage in the romantic adventure and chivalric style of European warfare, some Irishmen wore decorative green plumes and feathers in their hats in honor of the Green Isle so far away.

The romantic concepts of chivalric warfare were about to be cruelly shattered by the harsh realities of modern warfare. After initial duty in Virginia around the Washington, D.C. area in late 1861, the Irish Brigade embarked on its greatest challenge to date, the Peninsula Campaign. One of the more realistic soldiers at this time was Pvt. Patrick Casey, Company B, Sixty-ninth New York. At the beginning of the Peninsula

Campaign, he scribbled a note and placed it in his blue uniform pocket just in case he was killed in battle: "My name is Patrick Casey, Co. B, Sixty-ninth Regiment, N.Y.S.V. Any one finding this note on my person when killed will please write a note to my wife, and direct it as follows: Mrs. Mary Casey, No. 188 Rivington-street, New York [City]." Private Casey was one of the first Irish Brigade soldiers to die during the Peninsula Campaign. When Casey's remains were buried in the dark soil of the Virginia Peninsula, few Irish soldiers present at the funeral could imagine how many more Brigade members would follow Casey's tragic fate in the years ahead. Nothing in the past, either in American or Irish history, had quite prepared these young Irishmen for the brutal realities and horrors that they were about to face in one of the bloodiest wars of the Nineteenth Century.

CHAPTER 2

The Peninsula Campaign

After the Confederacy failed to exploit the success won at First Bull Run by making an attempt to capture Washington D.C., the North began to muster its considerable strength for a war in earnest. The North prepared to unleash a massive offensive against the Confederate capital of Richmond, Virginia. The promising West Pointer who conceived this campaign plan, General George B. McClellan, had already garnered a lofty reputation across the North as the "Young Napoleon."

General McClellan, commanding the Army of the Potomac, envisioned the possibility that one bold offensive might end the rebellion by the summer of 1862. On the Virginia Peninsula and from the beginning to the end of the campaign to capture Richmond, McClellan and his top lieutenants would come to rely repeatedly on the aggressiveness and combativeness of the Irish Brigade, especially when facing a crisis situation. After months of intense training, the Irish Brigade soldiers felt fully prepared for the upcoming challenge in Virginia.

Union Gen. George B. McClellan and his wife.

A vast armada of Union warships and troop transports pushed south down Chesapeake Bay to initiate the spring campaign of 1862. After successful amphibious landings on the isolated Virginia peninsula southeast of Richmond, the narrow finger of land nestled between the James River to the south, and York River to the north, in March and early April 1862, the huge invading army of "Little Mac" marched northwest toward Yorktown, Virginia, the site where George Washington and his French allies forced the surrender of an entire British army in 1781.

Meagher's soldiers were about to learn some hard lessons about the harsh realities of modern warfare as the Peninsula Campaign would be the first opportunity for the majority of Irish Brigade troops to engage in combat.

When the Confederates evacuated Yorktown, the Army of the Potomac, including the Irish Brigade, pursued the retreating Southerners northwest. With their weapons shouldered, the Irish soldiers slogged along the muddy roads leading to Richmond, passing through the bright green forests of the peninsula.

But McClellan wasted too much time before advancing on Richmond to initiate the spring campaign. Indeed, after having landed on the Virginia Peninsula, McClellan had outflanked the primary Confederate Army at Manassas west of Washington, D.C., forcing Gen. Joseph E. Johnston to hurriedly shift the Confederate army south before the mighty

JACKSON

Virginia Central R.R.

Pamunkey River

Mechanicsville, 26 June

PORTER
V CORPS

JOHNSTON / LEE

Gaines' Mill, 27 June

Richmond & York River R.R.

Oak Grove,
25 June

SUMNER
II CORPS

FRANKLIN
VI CORPS

Richmond

KEYES
IV CORPS

HEINTZELMAN
III CORPS

Savage's Station, 29 June

McCLELLAN

Seven Pines,
31 May-1 June

Richmond & Petersburg R.R.

White Oak Swamp, 30 June

Chickahominy River

Glendale, 30 June

CHAFFIN'S
BLUFF

DREWRY'S
BLUFF

Malvern Hill, 1 July

Harrison's Landing

James River

SEVEN DAYS' BATTLES
25 JUNE–1 JULY 1862

Ten Miles

A group of Irish Brigade members at Harrisons Landing close to the James River.

Army of the Potomac could push aggressively toward Richmond. Johnston succeeded in reaching the peninsula before McClellan pushed northwest in an effort to overwhelm Richmond. The open back door to Richmond slammed shut before the dilatory McClellan could enter.

With both armies facing each other, Johnston and McClellan maneuvered over the rain-drenched landscape in a tactical chess game to decide the possession of Richmond. Whenever McClellan maneuvered the Army of the Potomac in slow, deliberate fashion, the Irish found time between marches to have fun. The officers of the Irish Brigade once set up a festive horse race.

Two esteemed generals served as the judges while the Irish celebrated the "Chickahominy Steeple-Chase" in enthusiastic fashion. The grand prize of this festive horse race was a "magnificent tiger-skin, presented by Gen. Meagher, the spoils of his own gun in Central America," when he was a filibuster.

As could be expected in continuing an Irish tradition, the Irish officers raced the best horses. These thoroughbred animals possessed distinctly Irish names in honor of the Green Isle so far away. Lt. Col. Patrick Kelly rode a fast horse with the Gaelic name of "Faugh-a-Ballagh," while Maj. James Quinlan who commanded the Eighty-eighth New York,

Confederate Gen. Joseph E. Johnston

owned a horse appropriately named "Tipperary Joe" after his native Irish county.

Then, with an added touch of typical Irish humor, a final race during the festivities was held between the little drummer boys. They rode the backs of unruly mules long accustomed to carrying supplies, not riders. The celebration was sobered by the outbursts of arms in the distance: the initial phases of the battle of Fair Oaks, or Seven Pines, resounded from the battlefield on the hot, humid afternoon of May 31.

Indeed, heavy fighting erupted in the pine forests and small fields hewed out of the dense forests along the Federal defensive lines in the Fair Oaks-Seven Pines sector when Johnston ordered a hard strike in an attempt to drive the invaders from the gates of Richmond. Making a sound tactical decision, Johnston attacked while the Union army was

A mass grave at Seven Pines with an estimated 400 dead.

divided by the rain-swollen Chickahominy River.

Heavy fighting resumed the next day as two Irish Brigade regiments, the Sixty-ninth and Eighty-eighth New York, were ordered to advance and reinforce the hard-pressed lines of blue. Eager for action and to establish a name for themselves on the battlefield, the Irish Brigade soldiers were about to receive their baptism of fire.

A chaplain of the unit never forgot the impressive sight of the surging Irish Brigade as they met "the advance of the Confederate troops[.] They came on en masse, presenting a bold front. All the faith and piety preached during the few previous months must now be put into practice[.] Our men of the Irish Brigade blessed themselves with more than ordinary fervor, offered a few fervent prayers to God and His Blessed Mother, and then, resigned to fate, they passed, even in the face of impending perils, an occasional joke, or quoted a line of poetry." In a disciplined advance, the Irishmen of the Sixty-ninth and Eighty-eighth New York charged with flashing bayonets and high spirits.

A nearby Union army surgeon, Dr. Thomas Ellis, watched the attack and never forgot the inspirational sight of the Irishmen going into battle as a unit for the first time: "There was the Irish Brigade in all the glory of a fair, free fight. Other men go into fights sternly or indifferently, but the only man who, after all, really loves it, is the green immortal Irishman. So there the brave lads, with Meagher at their head, laughed, fought, and joked as though it were the finest fun in the world."

After charging several hundred yards, the two New York regiments suddenly halted on open ground just north of the Richmond & York River Railroad leading into Richmond. With a clatter of gear, the Irishmen in blue hurriedly formed into neat ranks, as if on the parade ground at Fort Schuyler. Once aligned in disciplined ranks, the Irish Brigade unleashed its first barrage into the advancing Rebels, knocking down groups of gray attackers.

Succeeding volleys from the two New York regiments broke the back of the southern onslaught, forcing the punished Confederates rearward. The Irishmen then surged forward south of the railroad, charging with bayonets. Meagher's New Yorkers poured over the iron tracks, then up a steep railroad embankment.

To inspire the Celtic warriors onward, Captain Clooney, former member of Meagher's Irish Zouaves of Company K, Sixty-ninth New York State Militia, mounted the railroad

Col. Robert Nugent, commander of the Sixty-ninth New York Infantry.

embankment with a banner. One Irish soldier later wrote how Clooney encouraged the troops forward while "bearing the green flag of the [Eighty-eighth New York] regiment in his hands, and waved it defiantly in the face and fire of the enemy." With fixed bayonets, the charging Irish stormed a Confederate defensive position in the thick timber east of Fair Oaks. Here, blue and gray met in close combat. Irish bayonets and musket-butts then swiftly eliminated the most stalwart Rebels.

This first battlefield success earned the Irishmen the praise of General McClellan. Indeed, these New York soldiers ensured that McClellan's blue lines held firm under the heavy pressure. A proud Col. Robert Nugent, who skillfully commanded the Sixty-ninth New York on June 1, correctly assessed how "Our fire was sustained with consistency until the enemy was silenced, and by checking the advance of the rebels had, I am inclined to believe, a marked effect on the fortunes of the day."

Meagher was overjoyed by the first success of the Irish Brigade. He described how "The fire of the two regiments was so telling that the enemy were compelled to retire, leaving their dead and wounded piled in the wood." Meagher's specific demand for his troops to be armed with the .69 caliber smoothbore musket had paid high dividends. Though considered obsolete by some experts when compared to the rifled musket, the .69 caliber smoothbore allowed them to use the deadly "buck & ball" ammunition at close range.

Father William Corby, who rode in front with Meagher and staff, dismounted during the battle to assist fallen Irishmen. The energetic chaplain of the Eighty-eighth New York gave the last rites to dying soldiers, while shots passed overhead. Demonstrating bravery on the battlefield endeared Chaplain Corby to the Irish soldiers. For the entire Irish Brigade, Father Corby served as an inspirational spiritual leader, in part because the common Irish soldiers equated their struggle to a righteous crusade. The Irish Brigade priests reinforced the Celtic soldiers' faith in themselves, Catholicism, and in the moral nature of their struggle.

Religion played a central role in the lives of the Irishmen, not only because of the cultural link to old Ireland, but also because Catholicism was seen as synonymous with Irish patriotism and nationalism. After the English invasion of Ireland, the Roman Catholic Church became a powerful emotional and psychological symbol of Irish freedom and independence against foreign occupation and oppression. The Catholic faith continued to inspire and motivate the Irish soldiers in blue in their struggle to win the war. The regimental chaplains of the Irish Brigade helped the soldiers endure the trials of combat and the hardships that became more bloody with each passing year.

Like other Irish Brigade chaplains, Father Corby cemented the already strong bond between Catholicism and patriotism. This fusion played a key role in fueling the high motivation and the fighting spirit of the men in the ranks. Such strong religious influences ensured that the Irish Brigade became the center of the Catholic faith in the Army of the Potomac. Father Corby explained, "the Irish Brigade was not entirely unworthy of the title of 'Headquarters' of the [Catholic] Church in the Army of the Potomac," mainly because most of the soldiers were Catholic.

Other priests of the Irish Brigade included Father James M. Dillion (Sixty-third New York), and Thomas Willet, who hailed from the French Catholic communities of lower Canada like Father Thomas Ouellet, the chaplain of the Sixty-ninth New York. Father Ouellet was a priest in service at St. John's College at Fordham, New York, when the war began. He became known for his courage under fire. Whenever "the bullets came thick and fast he was there, and paid no attention to the danger, announcing that he was not only a soldier of McClellan's army, but that he was also a soldier of Christ." Father Corby also possessed lower Canada roots in the Roman Catholic communities of the French. Corby's mother was born in Montreal and his Ireland-born father had migrated from Kings County, Ireland, to Canada, before migrating to the United States to start a new life.

While other unit chaplains would come and go, Corby, Dillion, and Ouellet would serve as a powerful and influential religious triumvirate that provided a solid religious foundation for the entire Irish Brigade. On both the battlefield and in the tented encampment, these hard-working Catholic chaplains bestowed spiritual guidance and comfort to the Irish fighting man.

The Twenty-ninth Massachusetts Volunteer Infantry joined the Irish Brigade not long after the battle of Seven Pines. This timely addition meant that the Irish Brigade was no longer an all-New York Irish Brigade. These hardy

New Englanders posed a problem when they joined the Irish Brigade as, unlike the almost all-Catholic New York regiments, the Massachusetts regiment was largely Protestant. As an indication of this new reality, the chaplain of the Twenty-ninth Massachusetts was a Protestant. The differences in religion ensured that the bond between the New York Catholics and the Massachusetts Protestants was never close.

Gen. Robert E. Lee, commander of the Army of Northern Virginia

Meanwhile, the war was about to enter a bloody new phase. President Davis appointed Gen. Robert E. Lee to command the Confederate forces defending Richmond after Johnston fell wounded at the battle of Seven Pines. The aggressive Lee resolved to deliver a succession of powerful blows upon the Army of the Potomac. These clashes outside Richmond would become known as the engagements of the Seven Days, the series of bloody battles lasting from June 25 to July 1.

After striking the Federals at Mechanicsville, Virginia, Lee's forces followed on the heels of the withdrawing Army of the Potomac to Gaines's Mill, northeast of Richmond. Lee then took advantage of the fact that the Army of the Potomac was divided by the flooded waters of the brown Chicka-hominy, and unleashed a massive assault north of the river. With Gen. Fitz John Porter's Fifth Corps, the Union army's vulnerable right wing, isolated north of the river, Lee assaulted Porter's corps at Gaines's Mill on June 27.

Union Gen. Fitz John Porter

To save the beleaguered Fifth Corps, McClellan hurriedly dispatched reinforcements from the south side of the river across the Chickahominy. The Irish Brigade was one of those reinforcing units ordered north across the river to bolster Porter's hard-hit corps at Gaines's Mill. The Irish Brigade troops were able to strengthen the wavering line and repel a Rebel attack, helping the heavily-pressured sector to hold firm under the heavy pressure.

Shocked by Lee's hard-hitting aggressiveness, McClellan slowly withdrew from the outskirts of Richmond because he feared that his army was vastly outnumbered. He then ordered his army south toward his newly chosen base on the James River where United States Navy gunboats could offer the army some protection. Fulfilling a vital role and once again demonstrating its dependability, the Irish Brigade helped to protect the withdrawal of the Army of the Potomac.

In striking contrast to the widespread demoralization among many Union troops, the Irish soldiers remained especially hopeful and optimistic about their chances for success in the next battle. To other Union commanders and their men, the Irish Brigade soldiers were well-known for their soaring morale that seemed to always remain high, regardless of the circumstances. In both English and Gaelic, the Irish soldiers often sang popular Irish ditties, such as "The Girl I Left Behind Me" and "Garry Owen," to lift each others spirits. At the time, the jaunty "Garry Owen" was the official regimental song of the Sixty-ninth New York.

Irish fiddlers, like diminutive Pvt. Johnny O'Flaherty, played traditional Irish tunes in the gloomy woodlands, clinging mud, and rains of the Virginia Peninsula. Irish Brigade members also played the ancient uilleann pipes. These traditional Irish pipes were similar to the better known Scottish bagpipes. To the Gaelic rhythms of ancient Irish melodies, Meagher's soldiers danced Irish jigs and reels nightly in the encampments. Other Irish soldiers sang songs such as "O'Connor's Bride," and "The Colleen Bawn." Many songs sung around the campfires were popular nationalist and political tunes, including "Fontenoy," and "The Green above the Red." Other popular songs of the Irish soldiers, especially the Fenians, were those that kept alive the memory of the great Irish Revolution of 1798. These patriotic tunes of the Irish nationalists included, "The Men of Ninety-Eight," "The Felons of Our Land," and "Brave General Munro."

For added entertainment and to the delight of the Irish soldiers in the ranks, young drummer boys often beat the popular tune, "St. Patrick's Day." Capt. David Power Conyngham explained how "knitted brows and a dark scowl marred their features, and their hands involuntarily grasped their muskets, as some powerful voice sang of the penal days and English oppression towards Ireland." Such patriotic songs of old Ireland not only fueled nationalist spirit but also provided a renewed sense of determination for the soldiers. Even the traditional Irish musical instruments, such as the uilleann pipes and harps, possessed a revolutionary significance for the Irish Brigade soldiers because the English had outlawed and hunted down Irish musicians who spread the faith of revolution and Irish freedom by way of popular songs

A hospital at Savage's Station on June 27, 1862.

and revolutionary lyrics. The camaraderie was strengthened by traditional Irish music, and common purpose kept the troopers' spirits high during the Union army's withdrawal to the James River.

More fighting erupted along the Richmond and York River Railroad at Savage's Station, directly east of Richmond when Lee again struck at McClellan's withdrawing army on June 29. This time, the Eighty-eighth and Sixty-ninth New York were held in reserve as the fighting roared to new heights of intensity. When the Rebels were beaten back by the resounding peals of gunfire, the opportunity developed to unleash a

The Union forces getting ready to leave Savage's Station.

counterattack. The ever-aggressive Meagher ordered the Irishmen forward.

With characteristic abandon and a distinctive Celtic cheer, the soldiers of the Sixty-ninth, Sixty-third, Eighty-eighth New York, and Twenty-ninth Massachusetts charged forward with flashing bayonets. The commander of the Twenty-ninth Massachusetts had his arm torn off by a cannonball, but his attacking New Englanders continued onward into the hail of fire. At the head of the Eighty-eighth New York, Maj. James Quinlan led his men up to the blazing guns of a Confederate battery. The bluecoat attackers swarmed the guns and battled hand-to-hand for possession of the coveted artillery pieces.

After killing or capturing the Confederate artillerymen, Meagher's victorious soldiers unleashed wild Irish cheers to celebrate their success. The entire Confederate battery would have been captured except that the Rebel gunners had hauled off some artillery pieces by hand to escape the surging blue tide of Irishmen.

Filling in for the regimental commander of the Eighty-eighth New York who had been stricken by disease, Quinlan proved to be a promising leader and a rising star in the Irish Brigade. He won a Medal of Honor for his courage at Savage's Station. The well-respected major was the first of eleven Irish Brigade members to receive the Medal of Honor.

The Irish Brigade soldiers were the last Union troops to evacuate the scene, serving yet again as the protective rear-guard for the hard-pressed Army of the Potomac as it continued to retire slowly south toward the James River. During this risky period for the withdrawing Union army, Meagher's troops continued to gain a reputation for reliability, especially during moments of crisis.

The Irish Brigade participated in another confrontation with aggressive Confederate forces on June 30 at White Oak Swamp when Meagher's Irishmen clashed with Stonewall Jackson's troops as Lee's Confederate forces continued to hammer the Army of the Potomac. Dr. Thomas Ellis witnessed the spirited advance of the Irish Brigade on this occasion: "The fiery brigade of Meagher dashed up gallantly on the right, using the musket quite soldierly." The Irish soldiers bolstered the front after rushing upon the field with cheers and bayonets at the ready. As on previous occasions, the Emerald Islanders ensured that the shaky blue lines would hold firm

A picture of the terrain that the Irish Brigade fought through at White Oak Swamp.

under the pounding. The Irishmen held steadfast in an exposed position before some of the finest troops of the Army of Northern Virginia. In the words of Lt. Richard Turner, "Our brigade was formed so as to support the battery—the four regiments in line—and then they lie down flat upon the ground, in order that the effect of the enemy's shell may be as ineffectual as possible[.] In this position the Brigade remains during the day, holding and sustaining the bridge at White

Oak Swamp," while protecting the sullen withdrawal of McClellan's forces. The guardian role played by the Irish soldiers in protecting the army's vulnerable rear ensured that the hard-pressed Army of the Potomac was able to safely retire south through White Oak Swamp with order and discipline.

The Irishmen also assisted in blunting the attack of Gen. James Longstreet's forces at the battle of Glendale. Here, at a key road junction three miles north of Malvern Hill and just south of White Oak Swamp, Lee continued to strike in repeated efforts to bring a decisive victory to the Confederacy by cutting McClellan's army in two. Yankee reinforcements, including the Irish Brigade, prevented that disaster by stabilizing the heavily-pressed Union lines.

Attempting to escape from the sledge-hammer-like blows of the past week and before Confederate forces could strike again, McClellan withdrew his army to Malvern Hill, the highest defensive ground just north of the James River and southwest of White Oak Swamp. Not only could the weary Army of the Potomac occupy the high ground, but the position could be supported by the considerable firepower of Federal gunboats in the nearby James River. After arriving before Malvern Hill, an impatient Lee launched a massive frontal assault on July 1, despite the position bristling with artillery,

The Confederate assaults were disjointed and piecemeal, minimizing their overall impact, though the relentless Rebel attacks did threaten to break through McClellan's defensive line on the left flank where Porter's Fifth Corps, weakened by the bloody fighting at Gaines's Mill, was vulnerable. A desperate Porter called for help from Gen. Edwin V. Sumner, who

Harper's Weekly *sketch of the Battle of Malvern Hill as it appeared in the July 26, 1862 issue.*

immediately dispatched the Irish Brigade to rescue the potentially disastrous situation. With a sense of urgency Meagher led the Irish Brigade forward on the double-quick, toward the point of greatest crisis on the field of Malvern Hill.

Along the way, the onrushing Irishmen unleashed their distinctive Gaelic yell, indicating their high spirits and eagerness for the fray. The commander of the Ninth Massachusetts Volunteer Infantry, composed of Boston Irish, watched the surging ranks of the Irish Brigade pass by, and "as they recognized a fellow country-man, they gave a yell that drowned the noise of the guns." One Confederate officer reacted to the noise by saying "Steady, boys, here comes that damned green flag again."

Members of the Sixty-ninth and Eighty-eighth New York charged south down the open slope of Malvern Hill to smash into an advancing line of Louisiana Rebels in a darkening wood-lot below the crest of Malvern Hill in the late afternoon. These opponents were the hard-fighting troops of the Tenth Louisiana Infantry, among them the famed Louisiana Tigers which consisted of a large percentage of New Orleans Irish. These two opposing units both possessed reputations as the hardest fighters in their respective armies. And now these soldiers in blue and gray met head-on at Malvern Hill in a dramatic showdown to prove which reputation would prevail and endure in the future.

A savage flurry of hand-to-hand combat erupted in the smoke-laced shadows of the trees. During the close-range fighting, an Irish "color-sergeant flaunts the flags at the rebels and falls [then] another grasps them and falls, and they are then borne by the corporals." The Irish Brigade was able to overwhelm these Confederate troops of Gen. Paul Jones Semmes's brigade and the momentum of the Irish charge forced the Rebels to retire northward in defeat. During the scrape, Pvt. Richard A. Kelly, Sixty-ninth New York, captured the lieutenant colonel of the Tenth Louisiana Regiment.

In helping to save the day at Malvern Hill, the Irish Brigade lost nearly 200 men. One Irishman killed in the bitter fighting was Capt. Joseph O'Donohue, a member of General Meagher's staff. He was serving as the acting major of the Eighty-eighth New York when he was killed. Only twenty-two, this "fine, soldierly-looking young man . . . had so many escapes that he had almost a Turkish belief in his good fortune, and looked upon himself as one of the fortunate, who were fated to pass scathless through the fiery ordeal of war," wrote Capt. David Power Conyngham, who served with O'Donohue on Meagher's staff. Pvt. Peter Rafferty, Company B, Sixty-ninth New York, was wounded and ordered rearward by his commander to the field hospital, but Rafferty refused to leave his busy comrades. He was hit several more times and then captured. For his courage, Rafferty received the Medal of Honor.

Not only at Malvern Hill, the last battle of the Peninsula campaign, but throughout the fighting on the Virginia Peninsula, the Irish soldiers performed in a manner that enhanced their reputation for combat prowess, steadfastness, and dependability on the battlefield, especially during crisis situations. As demonstrated repeatedly, bayonets were the "favorite weapons of war, so dreaded by the enemy, especially when accompanied by the green flag." The Irish Brigade's reputation for superior combat performances had even infiltrated the ranks of the Army of Northern Virginia by this time. One captured Confederate swore in grim resignation, "The Irish fight like devils!" The price for this burgeoning reputation was frightfully high. A member of the Eighty-eighth New York wrote: "Our heroic brigade left 700 of its bravest officers and men on the bloody fields [of the Peninsula campaign] behind."

The Irish Brigade's fame as an elite combat unit spread across the North, inspiring many Irish men, women, and children with a new sense of pride in themselves and their distinctive Celtic heritage and culture. General McClellan was especially thankful to the Irish Brigade for its protective

Union Gen. George B. McClellan's staff.

guardian role during the Peninsula Campaign, stating with sincerity to Meagher, "I wish I had twenty thousand more men like yours." News of the battlefield performance of the Irish soldiers even reached the White House and President Lincoln. In early July 1862, President Lincoln made a special visit to the Irish Brigade's encampment during his inspection of the Army of the Potomac. Unlike his increasingly negative personal views of McClellan, the president thought highly of Meagher. In an emotional tribute, the president kissed the bullet-riddled green battle-flag of the Sixty-ninth New York and proclaimed "God Bless the Irish Flag!" Captain

Conyngham described how, "The regimental flags were of a deep rich green, heavily fringed, having in the centre a richly embroidered Irish harp, with a sunburst above it and a wreath of shamrock beneath[.] Underneath, on a crimson scroll, in Irish characters, was the motto, 'They shall never retreat from the charge of lances.'" The emerald green flags represented something sacred to the Irish Brigade soldiers and, despite considerable efforts, the Confederates never captured the Irish Brigade's flag. In addition, the Irish regiments also carried the national colors, but flew no state flags like other Union regiments. Proving to be a strong component in psychological warfare that caused front-line Confederates a good deal of apprehension, the green flags possessed a power to shake the confidence of even the best Southern troops. Pvt. William McCarter of the 115th Pennsylvania wrote with amazement how "the emblem of the little Emerald Isle over the sea [was] the Green flag so feared, dreaded, and shunned by the Rebs. . . ."

It was appropriate that President Lincoln asked for God's blessings upon the Irish Brigade because the unit was about to face its greatest challenge to date, the Maryland Campaign. As if knowing that the greatest test by fire loomed on the horizon, Meagher returned to New York City during the summer of 1862 and began recruiting additional Irishmen to replenish the depleted ranks of his command. This recruiting mission was both timely and necessary, because the Peninsula Campaign had so severely culled the Irish Brigade's ranks.

Just before the defeat of Gen. John Pope's troops at the battle of Second Bull Run at the end of August, the Irish Brigade and other Army of the Potomac units were hurriedly recalled from the Virginia Peninsula to protect Washington, D.C. from the threat of Lee's army. In characteristic fashion, Lee pounced upon Pope at Second Bull Run and delivered yet another major defeat to the Union army at the same location where the Confederacy won its first major victory the previous summer. The Southerners' success opened the door for Lee to lead his army farther north across the Potomac River in the Confederacy's first invasion of the North. At the same time, Confederate forces started dual offensives in the West: the invasion of Kentucky and a thrust into northeastern Mississippi. With three different rebel offensive efforts moving northward, the summer of 1862 signaled the high tide of the Confederacy in both the eastern and western theaters.

CHAPTER 3

The War's Bloodiest Day: Attacking the Sunken Road at Antietam

After thousands of Confederates of Lee's Army crossed the shallow waters of Potomac River during four days in early September 1862, McClellan began a belated pursuit of the invaders in gray and butternut. With muskets on right shoulders and singing the traditional songs of old Ireland, the Celtic warriors of the Irish Brigade marched north with the rest of the Army of the Potomac to meet the great challenge of confronting Lee's invasion of the North. General McClellan had already worked wonders in forging a new fighting force from General Pope's defeated army and his own Army of the Potomac. Most important, he had been successful in lifting morale and getting the combined Union forces organized and ready for the Maryland Campaign.

Lee decided that Harpers Ferry and Martinsburg, Virginia, lying across his supply and communications line, had to be captured. Consequently, Lee, who had erroneously believed that the Union garrison at Harpers Ferry would evacuate its position, dispatched two-thirds of his already depleted army to capture Harpers Ferry. Meanwhile, the remainder of the Army of Northern Virginia pushed northwest from Frederick, Maryland, to cross the Catoctin Mountains and then the South Mountain chain of the Blue Ridge Mountains farther west.

So far, Lee's initiative had caught the Lincoln government and the Army of the Potomac unprepared for the invasion of Maryland. McClellan and his army had to play catch-up. But that tactical situation was about to change. McClellan was presented the opportunity of a lifetime and perhaps the greatest intelligence coup of the Civil War, when some homespun Indiana soldiers found a copy of Lee's campaign orders left behind in an abandoned Confederate encampment. These high-level orders indicated how widely-scattered and vulnerable was the Army of Northern Virginia at this time.

Soon, McClellan had the "lost" orders in his own hands. With renewed confidence, McClellan now set his army in pursuit of the Southerners northwest from Frederick, hoping to overwhelm the widely divided columns of the Army of Northern Virginia in short order, before they united.

Between the two armies lay the barrier of South Mountain. Employing masterful delaying tactics at the three gaps of South Mountain, the rear-guard Rebels stood firm in facing the Union army's determined attempt to swarm through the vital passes. Although the Army of the Potomac eventually dislodged the Rebel defenders, the defensive action allowed the Confederates precious time to concentrate their scattered forces along a slight ridge before the little western Maryland village of Sharpsburg. Here, on the

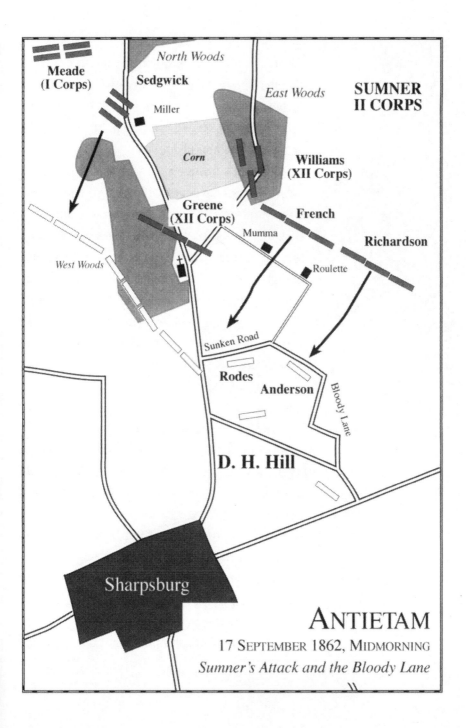

Meade
(I Corps)

North Woods

Sedgwick

Miller

East Woods

SUMNER
II CORPS

Corn

Williams
(XII Corps)

Greene
(XII Corps)

French

Mumma

Richardson

West Woods

Roulette

Sunken Road

Rodes

Anderson

Bloody Lane

D. H. Hill

Sharpsburg

ANTIETAM

17 SEPTEMBER 1862, MIDMORNING

Sumner's Attack and the Bloody Lane

Brig. Gen. Israel B. Richardson led the Union division that the Irish Brigade was a part of during the Battle of Antietam where he was killed.

west side of Antietam Creek, Lee made his stand. Ever the risk-taker, he now hoped for the arrival of General "Stonewall" Jackson's divisions from Harpers Ferry, before the powerful Army of the Potomac could advance to crush his divided army.

Meagher's brigade was part of Brig. Gen. Israel B. Richardson's division of Maj. Gen. John Sumner's II Corps. The fast-moving Irish Brigade led the westward pursuit of Lee's forces. In his battle report, a proud General Meagher wrote that, "the Irish Brigade had the honor of leading the pursuit of the rebels from South Mountain through [the small towns of] Boonsborough and Keedysville. Along this road and through these villages, in this pursuit, the brigade passed with the utmost alacrity and enthusiasm."

McClellan's army raced toward the small town of Sharpsburg hoping to strike Lee a blow that could cripple his army, before the arrival of Jackson's troops from Harpers Ferry. Upon nearing Sharpsburg, Meagher noted that the Federals were surprised when "the enemy were discovered in full force, drawn up in line of battle on the heights near Sharpsburg and overlooking the Antietam."

Throughout September 16, the ever-cautious McClellan missed a golden opportunity to destroy the weakened Army of Northern Virginia before it was completely united. The dramatic showdown in the valley of Antietam came the following day, September 17, 1862.

Drawing by Arthur Lumley depicting the Irish Brigade during the fighting of September 17, 1862.

The climactic battle erupted at first light. McClellan hurled a powerful sledgehammer blow of three corps southward against Lee's left, just north of Sharpsburg. Nightmarish fighting exploded in the North, East, and West Woods in the early morning hours. But the struggle was most severe in the David R. Miller cornfield. In this small cornfield of thirty acres sandwiched between the North, East and West Woods, blue and gray were slaughtered at unprecedented levels. As if sickened by the carnage, both sides broke off the contest out of sheer exhaustion by mid-morning.

After the morning phase of the day long struggle finally began to die down, the next phase of the battle of Antietam erupted. McClellan launched an attack on Lee's center using Sumner's Second Corps. Maj. Gen. William French, commanding the First Division, Second Corps, veered south toward the Confederate position in a recessed lane, at the center of Lee's thin battle-line, instead of supporting the advance of its sister unit, John Sedgwick's division. Sumner sent Sedgwick to assist Hooker's men on the East Woods, but French did not follow. Thus French's southbound attacks edged eastward, and that sent Richardson's division still further east and straight into the heart of the Confederate defense, a sunken road that was about to earn the infamous name "Bloody Lane."

For the stiff challenge that lay ahead, the Irish regiments were fortunate to be led by a group of fine officers of exceptional promise and ability. Leading the Sixty-ninth New York was Lt. Col. James Kelly, who hailed from Monaghan, Ireland. He had taken command of the regiment when Colonel Nugent became sick. Kelly possessed plenty of experience as a United States regular and as a member of the Sixty-ninth New York State Militia.

Reliable and steady Col. John Burke, a strict disciplinarian and "a splendid tactician," commanded the Sixty-third New York. The Ireland-born Burke was "the chief means of bringing the regiment to the high place it attained as a well-disciplined battalion."

Meanwhile, the Eighty-eighth New York, was led by the popular Lt. Col. Patrick Kelly. Kelly was a former private of the Sixty-ninth New York Militia. He had survived the battle of First Bull Run and the bitter fighting of the Peninsula Campaign, Patrick Kelly had been born in County Galway in west Ireland.

The Twenty-ninth Massachusetts Volunteer Infantry was under the capable leadership of Lt. Col. Joseph Barnes. He

had taken command of this regiment after the fall of the regimental commander at Savage's Station. These New
Englanders were determined to live-up to the lofty reputation
won by the three New York regiments during the bloody battles of the Peninsula Campaign.

Meanwhile, the Union brigades of General French's
Division assaulted the troops of Gen. Daniel Harvey Hill's
division and Gen. Richard H. Anderson's Division positioned
in the Sunken Road, a natural trench of formidable strength.
This excellent defensive position, amid the rolling and
sprawling fields, was now the center of Lee's thin battle-line.
As could be predicted when advancing across open ground in
parade-ground fashion against a strong defensive position,
these first attacking units of French's Division were repulsed
by the rolls of musketry pouring from the Sunken Road. The
beaten Yankee soldiers retired to escape the leaden storm,
leaving the bloody debris and human wreckage in the open,
plowed fields before the sunken road.

It was now the turn of Richardson's Division to attempt to
overwhelm the deceptively strong Confederate position. By
this time, the Sunken Road had now become the focal point of
the struggle during the second phase of the battle.

The Irish Brigade moved steadily toward the enemy's
strongest defensive position: the low-lying, narrow roadbed
made even more formidable by a fence rail breastwork hasti-
ly erected by the Alabama and North Carolina soldiers, who
knew how to fight and kill Yankees.

After the 1,400 soldiers of the Irish Brigade had pushed
forward for hundreds of yards across the wide, open fields of
the Samuel Mumma and William Roulette farms, Meagher

halted the Brigade to dress the lengthy ranks of blue. Meanwhile, a handful of volunteers dashed forward to tear down a long split-rail-fence, about 300 yards before the Confederate strong point and standing athwart of the advance.

All the while, deadly North Carolina and Alabama sharpshooters fired from tree tops along the Sunken Road, inflicting casualties among the Irish volunteers exposed in the sun-baked fields of Washington County. Among volunteers who pulled down the rail fence before the lengthy Irish formations was Pvt. Samuel Wright, Company E, Twenty-ninth Massachusetts Volunteer Infantry. Private Wright was especially conspicuous during this risky mission and won a Medal of Honor for his valor.

Additional Irish soldiers, meanwhile, began to drop in the wide open fields before the Sunken Road. The Irish Brigade soldiers were now beginning to realize that they had marched into a hornets' nest. Once the rail fence was knocked down, Meagher galloped to the Irish Brigade's front. He then yelled above the din of battle, "Irish Brigade! raise the colors and follow me!"

Meagher would not order his men to go where he would not go. If the Irish Brigade had a father, it was General Meagher.

As one, hundreds of Irishmen advanced with determination, while the green flags of Ireland waved overhead in the bright sunshine. The Irish soldiers advanced with .69 caliber smoothbores at the ready. These smoothbores were loaded with slightly smaller caliber balls to accommodate the three small buckshot to ensure a shotgun-like blast effect that could knock down multiple opponents with one blast, unlike the standard issue Springfield rifled-muskets with the .58 caliber minie ball.

Meagher developed a battle-plan to accomplish what one Union brigade after another had failed to achieve this morning, overwhelming the Sunken Road. He told his officers that the Irish Brigade soldiers were to deliver two volleys into the Sunken Road defenders and then unleash a bayonet attack.

Meagher encouraged his advancing Irishmen onward with the promise to Col. James Kelly, Sixty-ninth New York, that stirred their emotions to new heights: "It will be Fontenoy again, Colonel, Fontenoy!"

But in reality, it could never be Fontenoy again, because the nature of warfare had changed so thoroughly since then. Indeed, not only the times, but also the weapons and tactics had changed dramatically in the last 117 years since that famous battle in Belgium. This was no longer the days of the Eighteenth Century and the Napoleonic Era, which were dominated by the short-range and inaccurate smoothbore musket like at Fontenoy. The Confederate soldiers now defending the sunken road were armed with rifled muskets, a far deadlier weapon in terms of both range, velocity, and accuracy. With these advances in arms technology, the tactical defensive had been greatly enhanced and as never before.

Unlike in the past, the kind of head-on bayonet charge that had been unleashed by the old Irish Brigade on the open plains of Fontenoy was no longer a guaranteed formula for tactical victory. By 1862, a bayonet charge against a strong defensive position manned by soldiers armed with modern weaponry was little more than folly. A bayonet assault now only ensured the slaughter and the attackers' repulse, almost regardless of their numbers.

Neither Meagher nor other Union leaders fully realized that an evolution in arms technology had already occurred to make the old traditional tactics, that once had been so successful, now obsolete. While Meagher was trapped by the legacy of the tactical realities of Fontenoy, the nineteenth-century Union commanders were equally indoctrinated by the overwhelming American success in the Mexican-American War and the lesson of warfare in the Napoleonic Era, before the advent of rifled muskets revolutionized modern warfare.

Closer and closer, meanwhile the Celtic soldiers advanced toward the sunken road. The closeness of the defiant Rebel banners indicated that a large number of defenders were packed together in the narrow roadway that now served as a perfect trench. Confederate veterans upon glimpsing hundreds of Irish soldiers, moving relentlessly toward them, not only marveled at the discipline and precision of Meagher's advance, but also knew that much serious hard fighting lay ahead.

Meanwhile, additional Irish soldiers began to drop to the ground, falling to the brisk fire from Confederate skirmishers, who could not miss at such a close range. Father Corby recalled: "I shall never forget how wicked the whiz of the enemy's bullets seemed as we advanced into that battle. As soon as my men began to fall, I dismounted and began to hear confessions on the spot. It was then I felt the danger even more than when dashing into battle."

Anderson's North Carolina brigade defended the right wing of the sunken road, while Rodes' Alabama brigade held the left wing. With cruel efficiency, hot fire from the Rebel skirmishers knocked more Irish Brigade soldiers out of the surging ranks of blue. Nevertheless, the neat formations of

Meagher's brigade, along with the rest of Richardson's division, continued to pour forward with flags flying.

Suddenly, on the Irish Brigade's left, a butternut-hued column from Gen. Carnot Posey's Mississippi brigade advanced from its defensive position. Posey's troops opened fire on the left flank of the Sixty-third New York. However, half a dozen well-directed volleys from the Sixty-ninth New York, and then the advance of Lt. Col. Patrick Kelly's Eighty-eighth New York and the Sixty-third New York eliminated the Mississippi threat as suddenly as it had appeared.

This accurate fire sent the Mississippians hustling back to gain the protection of the Sunken Road. Also fleeing for safety were the pesky Rebel skirmishers. They were hurled rearward by the advancing ranks of the Irish Brigade. Quickly eliminating the Mississippians' threat ensured that the Irish Brigade's advance could maintain proper alignment, and continue forward in a unified manner to deliver the maximum blow upon the defenders. Four regiments of Anderson's veteran brigade lay under the good cover of the sunken lane. They waited for the dense blue ranks of the Irish Brigade to gain the crest of the slight rise located just before the low-lying road.

Because the Sixty-ninth New York occupied the right flank of the Irish Brigade, and advanced across lower-lying terrain that dipped into the depression where the Roulette farm lane intersected the mid-point of the sunken road, this unit was the first Irish Brigade regiment to be exposed to fire from the sunken road. The rebels opened a scorching fire on the Sixty-ninth New York, as soon as these New Yorkers gained the crest to reveal themselves as ideal targets. This first fire delivered at close range was severely punishing, rippling down the

Col. John B. Gordon, commander of the Sixth Alabama at the Sunken Road.

ranks of the Sixty-ninth New York with the force of a tornado.

Lifting the fighting spirit of the entire Irish Brigade, the Celtic soldiers, without having to be ordered to do so, unleashed a spontaneous and rhythmic chant, as the majority of the Irish troops neared the crest before the Sunken Road. For the first time in their lives, the men from North Carolina heard words of Gaelic from a far-away land across the sea. Rising above the escalating roar of battle, the unforgettable Irish chant of "Faugh-a-Ballagh!," echoed over the fields of death.

The fighting spirit demonstrated by the Irish soldiers acted like a tonic to other Federal troops. The effect of the Irish cheers fortified the resolve of a good many other Yankees of French's division, which had been hard-hit. Survivors of the previous bloodied attacks likewise began to cheer in response to the Gaelic war-cries. Then, the rallied troops advanced to resume the fight beside the Irish soldiers. All the while, the lengthy ranks of the Irish Brigade kept moving forward with Meagher leading the way. Some Celtic soldiers became shaky and lost their nerve, after having passed over the increasing numbers of dead and wounded bluecoats of the last failed attack.

Like the Irish Brigade troops, the Alabama and North Carolina defenders of the Sunken Road were highly motivated. Commanding the Sixth Alabama that occupied the right flank of the Alabama brigade, Col. John B. Gordon, a

University of Georgia graduate, wrote that "Gen. Lee had decided that the Union commander's next heavy blow would fall upon our centre, and those of us who held that important position were notified of this conclusion [and were determined] to hold that centre at any sacrifice, as a break at that point would endanger his entire army."

Finally, the other three regiments of the Irish Brigade surged to the crest, topping the high ground that loomed only a short distance before the Sunken Road.

A sweeping volley from hundreds of muskets of the Second, Fourth, Fourteenth, and Thirtieth North Carolina exploded in the faces of the Irish soldiers, when the Rebels rose up and fired as one. A solid flame leaped from the bowels of the Sunken Road, as a sheet of musketry rippled along the massed gray and butternut-hued ranks. A torrent of minie balls ripped through the blue formations of the Irish Brigade. Irish soldiers dropped in clumps, along with their green flags. Maj. Richard O. Bentley, Sixty-third New York and a native of Albany, New York, described the horror in a letter: "a single volley [succeeded in] cutting down nearly the whole [left] wing" of the Irish Brigade. Major Bentley was soon hit, and seriously wounded.

One color bearer after another was shot down while carrying the green battle-flag of the Sixty-ninth New York. Despite bullet holes cut through his uniform and so many of his men shot down, Meagher yelled, "Boys, raise the colors, and follow me!" In total, a dozen color bearers of the Sixty-ninth New York were cut down on this bloody day.

One of the few higher ranking Irish Brigade officers to survive the slaughter, Lt. Col. Henry Fowler, was appalled by the carnage: "The killed died as brave men, sword in hand, and amid the thickest of the fight . . . Our number now left less than 50 men; our colors, although in ribbons, and staff shot through, were still there, sustained at a bloody sacrifice" of more than a dozen color bearers.

Despite the shock of the volume of fire pouring from the sunken road and with so many men shot down, the Irish soldiers gamely held their advanced positions. They maintained these exposed positions before the Rebel firing line from the relative low ground just east of the Roulette Lane eastward for around 300 yards, while the slight ridge-line, running parallel to the Sunken Road, rose higher to the west. Amid the open fields, this lengthy line of Irish soldiers stood shoulder-to-shoulder as if on a parade ground or a drill field, while returning a hot fire into the Sunken Road defenders. All the while, more Irishmen fell to the ground, dropping like autumn leaves in far-away Ireland.

The fighting spirit of the Irishmen remained intact amid the carnage of the rapid exchange of gun-fire with the Sunken Road defenders. Blue and gray fought within a stone's throw of each other. By "this time the color-bearer in the right wing advanced several paces to the front, and defiantly waved his flag in the faces of the enemy: as if by a miracle, he escaped without serious injury." Meagher prepared to launch and lead a bayonet charge in a desperate bid to yet overwhelm the Confederate defenders.

However, larger numbers of Irish soldiers continued to drop, with the punishing fire erupting from the Sunken Road and pile of fence rails growing in intensity. After riding over to encourage the Eighty-eighth New York, on the left flank,

The dead at the Sunken Road.

forward with the bayonet, General Meagher went down hard, when his horse was shot from under him. He was knocked unconscious by the fall. Meagher was carried rearward by his boys, before additional Rebel bullets could claim the life of the father of the Irish Brigade.

The scorching gunfire exploding from the Confederate position was too murderous to endure by any soldiers. The Irish Brigade's last attempt to carry the Sunken Road with the bayonet came to a bloody end, with the bodies of more Irish soldiers piling higher under the searing musketry and burning sun of mid-September.

In the hail of lead, all of General Meagher's staff were either killed or wounded. The deadly duel between the Irish soldiers and the North Carolina Rebels continued for what seemed like an eternity, with both sides exchanging a blistering fire. Men loaded and fired as rapidly as possible, trying to kill as many of their opponents as possible. Not about to give up the fight, the Twenty-ninth Massachusetts and other Irish Brigade troops launched a bayonet attack in a last desperate attempt to overwhelm the tenacious Confederate defense in the lane.

Near the right-center of the Irish Brigade, the crest of the slight ridge before the Sunken Road rose to form a knoll. This knoll was the highest terrain feature immediately before the Rebel line. The top of the knoll was the key to the battlefield at this point.

This elevated perch allowed the Irish soldiers to turn their smoothbore muskets to the right, or westward, to enfilade the exposed right of the Alabama brigade. This blazing fire raked Colonel Gordon's Sixth Alabama, which anchored the right flank of the Alabama brigade. The Sixth Alabama was especially vulnerable, lying in the lower ground of the Sunken Road as it descended into a shallow hollow to meet the Roulette farm lane. This point was the only weak link in the otherwise powerful Confederate defensive line along the Sunken Road. This situation offered a tactical advantage for

Meagher's soldiers, who exploited the opportunity by directing an enfilade fire into the exposed lane.

At this time, the shotgun effect of the Irish soldiers' "buck
and ball" rounds was especially devastating, sweeping the
length of the Sixth Alabama's position with a vengeance.
Colonel Gordon was wounded and more of his men piled up
like cordwood in the narrow roadbed. Now, it was the turn of
the "Bloody Lane" Rebels to be slaughtered, as they had
slaughtered the Irish soldiers on the open fields before them.

Gordon was finally knocked out of action for good, when
he fell with his fifth wound. When his wife, fearing he had
been mortally wounded, later reached his bedside, the cheer-
ful colonel would quip, without fully realizing how appropriate was his analogy: "Here's your handsome husband; been
to an Irish wedding."

At last, under so much punishment from the flank fire
delivered from the Irishmen atop the knoll and just before the
ammunition of Meagher's men had been expended, the Sixth
Alabama could take no more punishment. Already piles of
Alabama soldiers lined the bottom of the lane. The right of
the Alabama brigade simply folded-up, collapsing under the
weight of the fire of the hard-fighting Celts in blue.

The Sixth Alabama's survivors fell back causing the other
Alabama regiments of General Rodes' brigade to its left to likewise withdraw, collapsing of the defensive line in Lee's center.
The Irish Brigade had played the key role in the overwhelming
of the Sunken Road. Col. John Burke, Sixty-third New York,
took command of what little remained of the bloodied brigade.

The price had been frightfully high. The Sixty-third New
York suffered 202 casualties, nearly 60 percent of its

Lt. Col. Henry Fowler, commander of the Sixty-third New York, with unknown officer.

strength, the greatest regimental loss of the Irish Brigade. Lieutenant Colonel Fowler, the acting commander of the Sixty-third, wrote that the initial Rebel volley "in an instant killed or wounded every officer but one and more than one-half the rank and file of the right wing." Nevertheless, the surviving Sixty-third soldiers kept loading and firing for hours, until they ran out of ammunition.

The Sixty-ninth New York suffered the second highest loss in the Irish Brigade, with a total of 196 men and officers killed or wounded. The Eighty-eighth New York lost a total of 104 soldiers. In his battle report, Lt. Col. Patrick Kelly, commanding the regiment, recalled, "I know not exactly how long we were in action, but we were long enough there to lose, in killed and wounded, one-third of our men (bringing in 302 and losing 104)."

Fortunate to have escaped the worst of the carnage and slaughter, the Twenty-ninth Massachusetts took losses of only 40 men. Nevertheless, the regiment from New England saw much hard fighting. The Twenty-ninth's Pvt. Samuel C. Wright was the only member of the Irish Brigade to win a Medal of Honor for heroics at Antietam.

All in all, the Irish Brigade lost a total of 113 killed, 422 wounded, and 5 missing, for a total of 450 casualties. These Celtic soldiers were cut down in only a few hours of fighting by the murderous fire pouring from "Bloody Lane."

Following the battle, the burial details of the Irish Brigade performed the sad task of burying its dead. Since General McClellan's army retained possession of the field of Antietam and the ever-cautious general decided not to pursue when General Lee and his beaten army slipped across the Potomac to the safety of Virginia, sufficient time remained to give the Irish dead a decent burial.

The Irish Brigade's high casualty rate in only a few hours of fighting at Antietam was not in vain. After the bloodiest day in American history, McClellan and his battered Army of the Potomac had repulsed Lee's first invasion of the north. More than 23,000 Americans on both sides fell in the single day's fighting. The Army of Northern Virginia's bid to win a decisive victory north of the Potomac was a failure.

With the political advantage open after Lee's army withdrew from western Maryland and back to Virginia, President Lincoln issued the Emancipation Proclamation, bestowing upon the Union war effort a new moral high ground that would never be relinquished. President Jefferson Davis's dream of gaining foreign recognition from the British, who wanted to see a permanently divided United States to ensure their own power, was thwarted by the Union victory at Antietam and by Lincoln's proclamation.

To the delight of Meagher's soldiers, the Irish Brigade had not only struck a blow against the Confederacy's bid at reap decisive political dividends with victory north of the Potomac, but also helped to drive a nail in Great Britain's global aspirations. For the Irish Brigade soldiers, this accomplishment was almost as rewarding as striking at British rule in Ireland.

Union Gen. Ambrose E. Burnside, commander of the Army of the Potomac.

What had died for the Irish Brigade at the Bloody Lane, in addition to more than 100 of its soldiers, was the romantic illusion that the Celtic soldiers would gain a succession of victories like Fontenoy and at a relatively low cost in lives. As demonstrated at Antietam, this struggle had evolved into a totally new kind of war quite unlike anything that could have been imagined by these Irishmen only a short time before. And this brutal conflict was about to become even bloodier in the days ahead for the Irish Brigade and the Army of the Potomac.

In the days after Antietam, Gen. Ambrose E. Burnside replaced McClellan because of his failure to destroy the Army of Northern Virginia. With Burnside came a fresh plan of offensive operations for the winter of 1862. A new campaign was born with the idea for an offensive drive across the Rappahannock to capture Fredericksburg before pushing south toward Richmond by land. The North sought to exploit the initiative gained in the bloody farms and fields of western Maryland.

Meanwhile, the exhausted Irish Brigade troops recuperated. On October 10, a new regiment joined the decimated Brigade at Harpers Ferry, Virginia. This new addition was the 116th Pennsylvania Volunteer Infantry. This fine Pennsylvania regiment had been organized by Col. Dennis Heenan, a fiery Irish commander, a skilled leader, who was well respected by the men in the ranks.

The under-strength 116th Pennsylvania, mostly from Philadelphia, retained a distinctly Irish and urban quality like the three New York regiments of the Irish Brigade. Early in the war, this unit had possessed sufficient Celtic identity to become known as the "Brian Boru United Irish Legion." More of the dominant Irish flavor of the 116th Pennsylvania was evident in the name of the sprawling encampment where it was organized, Camp Emmet. This encampment was named in honor of the Irish revolutionary, Robert Emmet, who had been executed in Dublin by the British in September 1803.

However, the 116th Pennsylvania also contained many Germans from the rural farming regions outside Philadelphia. The bluecoats of this regiment sang more popular wartime songs of the Union, such as "John Brown's Body," and "The Star Spangled Banner," than the troops of the Irish Brigade, where the traditional songs of old Ireland could be heard. The Pennsylvanians were armed with the .58 caliber Springfield rifled musket, while the remainder of the Irish Brigade troops were armed with the .69 caliber smoothbore musket.

Lt. Col. St. Clair Augustin Mulholland, commander of the 116th Pennsylvania, Irish Brigade.

The Twenty-ninth Massachusetts was transferred to another brigade, leaving the Irish Brigade much more thoroughly Irish and Catholic. Many of the New Englanders were Protestants, one reason why they had refused Meagher's offer to fight under a green flag. They felt that the emerald green color represented Fenianism and not old Ireland. This was partly correct because the spirit of Fenianism, especially among the higher ranking officers of the Irish Brigade, was a factor that fueled the fighting spirit of the Irish Brigade.

Feeling honored to join the Irish Brigade, Lt. Col. St. Clair A. Mulholland, commanding the 116th Pennsylvania, wrote: "The brigade to which the regiment had been assigned was a celebrated one, renowned for hard fighting and famous fun . . . The very name of this brigade was redolent of dash and gallantry, of precision of evolution and promptness of action; [it] was often referred to as Meagher's Brigade."

Other soldiers of the 116th Pennsylvania felt the same. A large percentage of Irish filled the ranks of the 116th Pennsylvania. This demographic included many of the officers, including Capt. John McNamara, who commanded Company E, Capt. Lawrence Kelly, who led Company G, and Capt. John O'Neill, who was in charge of Company K.

Pvt. William McCarter, a twenty-one-year-old Irish immigrant of the 116th Pennsylvania, was impressed not only by the Irish Brigade soldiers, but also their leader, General Meagher. He wrote: "In personal appearance, Gen. Meagher was about 35 years old, five feet-eight or ten inches high, of rather stout build, and had a clear high-colored complexion. He wore a heavy, dark brown moustache, closely trimmed. Except in battle, where he generally wore only the uniform of a private soldier, he nearly always appeared in the full dress of his rank [and] In thorough military skill and in courage and bravery on the battlefield, he was second to none in the Army of the Potomac . . . In kindness and thoughtfulness for his men, he was the shining light and bright star of the whole Union Army [and] made unceasing efforts to have his soldiers all well provided for and made comfortable . . . He was one of the very few military leaders who never required or would ask any of his command to go where he would not go himself. Meagher was first to lead the way."

To further compensate for the Twenty-ninth Massachusetts's departure, the Irish Brigade was bolstered by another New England regiment from the same state, the Twenty-eighth Massachusetts Volunteer Infantry, on November 23, 1862. The Twenty-eighth Massachusetts had been organized in the fall of 1861 at Cambridge, Massachusetts, just outside Boston. The Irish Brigade finally possessed the strength of five regiments like most other brigades of the Army of the Potomac.

The Twenty-eighth Massachusetts was not only a veteran regiment but also contained far more Irish Catholics than the Twenty-ninth Massachusetts. And this New England unit was as much Catholic and Irish as the three New York regiments of the Irish Brigade. So many Irish filled its ranks that the regiment was unofficially known by the men in the ranks as the Second Irish Regiment of Massachusetts.

Unlike the rest of the Irish Brigade soldiers who were armed with trusty .69 smoothbore muskets, these hardy New Englanders carried .577 caliber Enfield rifles. This firearm was the same deadly rifled weapon that had cut down so many Irish soldiers at Antietam. The third highest ranking officer of the Twenty-eighth Massachusetts was young George W. Cartwright, who had been born in Dublin. His father, Thomas W. Cartwright, commanded a company of the Sixty-third New York. The addition of the Twenty-eighth Massachusetts to the Irish Brigade resulted in an emotional reunion between father and son.

By any measure, the Twenty-eighth Massachusetts was a most worthy addition to the Irish Brigade. Its commander, Col. Richard Byrnes, was as tough as nails. He was an old United States Army regular who had served as sergeant-major of a cavalry regiment in prewar days. Possessing more than a dozen years of hard-earned experience, Byrnes had been badly wounded in fighting Native Americans on the western frontier. By this time, Byrnes was a strict taskmaster who knew exactly how to mold his Massachusetts regiment into a well-honed fighting machine.

The depleted Irish Brigade would need such sturdy fellow Irishmen and kindred spirits in its ranks for the upcoming battlefield challenge. The Twenty-eighth Massa-chusetts became the largest regiment of the Irish Brigade, with more than 400 soldiers. They were a most welcomed addition to an Irish Brigade devastated by the ravages of disease and high losses in one battle after another. While Antietam witnessed the bloodiest day in American history, the next battle was destined to be the bloodiest day in the Irish Brigade's history.

CHAPTER 4

"Never were men so brave:" Fredericksburg

Irish Brigade soldiers expected to spend the winter of 1862-1863 at their comfortable winter encampment at Falmouth, Virginia, just north of Fredericksburg. As was customary, the next fighting was expected with the opening of the spring campaign of 1863. In the words of Private McCarter, 116th Pennsylvania: "The men anticipated spending what many of them termed 'a gay and happy winter in Dixie's land'. But alas, poor fellows, hundreds never left the place. Such is the fate of war."

General Burnside planned to embark upon a new overland campaign in winter to drive south to capture Richmond. In the first phase of this new offensive, Burnside decided to launch an attempt to capture Fredericksburg, located about halfway between Washington, D.C. and Richmond. His first task would be to transfer his vast army to the west side of the Rappahannock River.

Marye's House in Fredericksburg, Maryland, close to where the Twenty-fourth Georgia fought the Irish Brigade.

But Lee was ready. He transformed Marye's Heights, the line of bluffs located in the rear of the colonial period town on the Rappahannock River, into a natural fortress. If Burnside crossed the Rappahannock and captured Fredericksburg, he would then be forced to attempt to gain the high ground that overlooked the town on the west side of the river.

Once again, the Army of the Potomac committed the folly of unleashing massive frontal assaults that had little, if any,

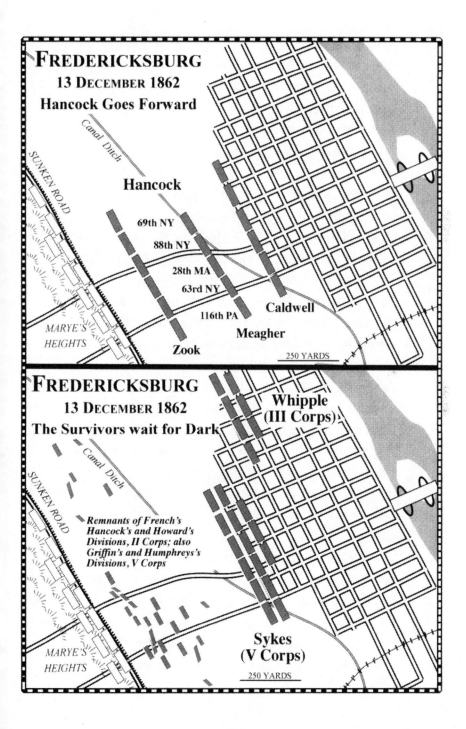

Fredericksburg
13 December 1862
Hancock Goes Forward

Canal Ditch

SUNKEN ROAD

Hancock

69th NY

88th NY

28th MA

63rd NY

116th PA

Caldwell

Meagher

Zook

MARYE'S HEIGHTS

250 YARDS

Fredericksburg
13 December 1862
The Survivors wait for Dark

Whipple
(III Corps)

Canal Ditch

SUNKEN ROAD

Remnants of French's Hancock's and Howard's Divisions, II Corps; also Griffin's and Humphreys's Divisions, V Corps

MARYE'S HEIGHTS

Sykes
(V Corps)

250 YARDS

chance for success, because of the superiority of the tactical defense over the tactical offensive. Indeed, the superiority of modern weaponry and the high ground defensive advantage were now paramount in warfare—a lesson yet unlearned by Burnside and most other Army of the Potomac commanders.

The challenge of Fredericksburg was most daunting. Looking at the Confederate fortifications from the east bank of the Rappahannock, Irish Brigade members dreaded the prospect of an assault. McCarter explained "It would be hard to describe the feelings of our boys in contemplating these gigantic preparations for the bloody and terrific contest which soon followed . . . . Suffice it to say that the almost general feeling among the Union troops was one of gloom and great depression. They saw before them the strong, almost impregnable position of the enemy . . . ."

Equally sobered by the challenge posed by Fredericksburg, Chaplain Corby described the looming obstacle now faced by the Irish Brigade and the Army of the Potomac: "we saw the city, and immediately behind the city the hills rising in terraces, in the form of a semi-circle, as if made by nature for a most impregnable position . . . the Confederates massed on the hills behind the city [and] built breastworks, and got all their heavy artillery in the best possible positions."

The Confederates had transformed the commanding heights behind Fredericksburg into a formidable defensive position. Father Corby and other veteran Irish Brigade soldiers could hardly imagine that Burnside would even contemplate committing the ultimate folly of hurling the Army of the Potomac against such a strongly fortified position as Marye's Heights.

Nevertheless, many Irish Brigade soldiers remained optimistic. Cpl. William A. Smith, Company D, 116th Pennsylvania, wrote that "we expect to go across the river . . . and take Fredericksburg [as] we have give[n] them orders to give up the town [but] they will not do it yet [and] so I expect the ball will open [soon and] we will make them dance . . . ."

After much difficulty, Union engineers finally completed construction of pontoon bridges across the Rappahannock. This engineering feat under fire of Mississippi sharpshooters in the town allowed the Army of the Potomac to cross to the river's west side and into Fredericksburg. As if an ill omen of the tragic events to come, a young drummer boy of the Irish Brigade lost his balance and slipped off the edge of the overcrowded bridge and fell into the cold waters of the Rappahannock. The young Irish lad immediately sank under the brown, swirling waters and drowned before anyone could reach him.

Once across the river, the Irish soldiers had little time to rest. Sgt. Welsh remembered how on the bitterly cold morning of December 13, "about eight oclock [*sic*] we were ordered to fall in and we were drawn up in line of battle in one of the streets [of Fredericksburg and] the enemy commenced to shell us . . . ."

While the Irish Brigade was poised amid the debris of a half-destroyed Fredericksburg, a rain of shells from Confederate artillery, aligned across Marye's Heights in imposing fashion, descended upon the bluecoat troops packed together in tight formations in the narrow streets, Capt. John Sullivan, Sixty-third New York, was marching his company down one of the cobblestone streets of

Fredericksburg, when suddenly "a cannon ball came bounding along, striking him in the leg and breaking the bone . . . ." Captain Sullivan, "a dashing, brave, and fearless soldier," was destined to die in only a few days. Other good fighting men, such as Lt. Seneca G. Willauwer, of the 116th Pennsylvania, fell to exploding shells. One shell killed and wounded eighteen soldiers of the Eighty-eighth New York. The Irish Brigade was severely punished by the accurate fire of the Confederate artillery on Marye's Heights. General Meagher's command lost 17 men killed, and another 26 wounded during the heavy artillery bombardment, "before even seeing a Rebel soldier," lamented Private McCarter.

Finally, the long-awaited order came to "Fall In!" Once again, the men of the Irish Brigade snapped to attention. Young Private McCarter never forgot that this fateful order "was the 'death-knell' to many a brave and loyal heart in the Irish Brigade . . ."

The Irish Brigade was among the second wave of attackers, after an initial Union assault was repulsed. Riding up on horseback, Meagher and his orderlies suddenly appeared before the lengthy lines of the Irish Brigade. McCarter described how the orderlies were "bearing in their arms large bunches of green boxwood [and then began to] present in [Meagher's] name a green sprig to each man in the ranks. They were to stick these bits of green in their caps before advancing against the enemy."

These sprigs of green now represented old Ireland, reminding and inspiring the Celtic soldiers to do their best today. Pvt. William H. McClelland, Eighty-eighth New York, wrote how General Meagher, who had three green sprigs of boxwood in his own hat, "gave us each a sprig of evergreen to put in our caps [and] We all looked gay and felt in high spirits, little dreaming, though we expected a heavy battle, that in so short a time after so many of our poor fellows would have been sent to their final doom."

Passing through the ruined town of Fredericksburg and moving out into the broad, open plain before Marye's Heights on this freezing Saturday, Burnside's forces deployed on level fields, devoid of cover or trees or brush, before the looming high ground. Here, around 1,200 Irish soldiers prepared for their greatest challenge to date, as evident by cartridge-boxes overflowing with 80 rounds, double the normal amount.

After the struggle for possession of "Bloody Lane" at Antietam, the green flags of the three New York regiments were so thoroughly cut to ribbons by Confederate bullets, that mere silken shreds of hung from flagstaffs. New green flags had been ordered from the Tiffany Company, New York, to replace the original banners but were not yet with the regiments. Meagher ordered the wearing of the sprigs of green boxwood to compensate for the missing emerald green battle flags.

At last, the Irish Brigade was ready to attack. The 116th Pennsylvania, Sixty-third New York, Twenty-eighth Massachusetts, Eighty-eighth New York, and the Sixty-ninth New York, were aligned from left to right. Because the newcomers from New England now carried the only green battle-flag in the entire Irish Brigade, Col. Byrnes and his Twenty-eighth Massachusetts were placed in the line's center. Meagher understood the psychological importance of the sight of the emerald green flag to inspire the Irish Brigade troops.

The Irish Brigade was about to attack across a lengthy stretch of wide open ground against yet another formidable defensive position made even stronger by a sunken road as at Antietam. Running along the base of Marye's Heights, this sunken road was known locally as the Telegraph Road. This sunken road was fronted by a sturdy stone wall, behind which stood hundreds of Confederate veterans.

To gain at least a small amount of protection from the heavy shelling, Meagher ordered his regiments to lie down on the ground while waiting for the order to attack. The Irish Brigade would have to wait its turn to assault the stone wall and sunken road. With the brief reprieve, Irish soldiers grasped rosary beads and crucifixes, praying that they would not have to attack the high ground covered with Confederate artillery and infantry.

At last, the order came to stand to attention. Hundreds of Irishmen suddenly rose as one with Meagher's order. Before the lengthy blue lines and mounted on his war-horse, Meagher then barked the command, "Fix Bayonets!" Pvt. William McCarter, long remembered how "the clink, clink, clink of the cold steel sounding along the line made one's blood run cold."

But rising even higher than the sharp clanging of the fixing of bayonets was the wild Gaelic cheering that accompanied the order to fix bayonets. "This was done amid the yells and cheers of the men, resounding from one end of the valley to the other." One vengeful Irishmen fixed his bayonet with the remark that revealed both hatred and contempt toward the thousands of veteran Confederates waiting to greet General Meagher's assault: "Damn them. That's the 'thing' [the bayonet] to fetch the sons of bitches."

The Irish Brigade now surged forward. From their high ground, the Southern artillery fire was punishing, ripping into and breaking apart the surging ranks of the Irish Brigade. Exploding Rebel shell knocked groups of Celtic soldiers from the advancing line. Maj. John Dwyer, Sixty-third New York, described how "canister shot, shrapnel, and shell ploughed the ground all round this devoted brigade, but they faltered not; they rushed on to their doom." The disciplined Irish Brigade troops simply closed ranks to fill the gaping holes in formations, and continued on toward the high ground. A soldier of the Eighth Ohio Volunteer Infantry never forgot the imposing sight of the Irish Brigade's charge and especially the attacking Irish soldiers, who had "a half-laughing, half-murderous look in his eye [and] They pass to our left, poor glorious fellows, shaking goodbye to us with their hats!"

Not only the green banner of the Twenty-eighth Massachusetts, decorated with the large gold harp of Ireland, but also the green sprigs of boxwood in the Celtic soldiers' hats allowed the Georgia Irishmen to recognize that their own fellow countrymen were surging toward them. Consequently, among the Confederates rose the lament before the killing began in earnest: "Oh God, what a pity! Here comes Meagher's fellows!" A Rebel wrote in a letter to his wife in the South: "Why, my darling, we forgot they were fighting us, and cheer after cheer at the fearlessness went up all along our lines" for the attacking Irishmen in blue.

In addition, the South Carolina and Georgia defenders of the stone wall and sunken road waved their hats and cheered the sight of the charging Irishmen from the far-away "old sod." After the spontaneous outburst of cheering, the Rebels sighted their Enfield rifles and smoothbore muskets on individual Celtic soldiers and waited for the signal to open fire. These Georgia and South Carolina veterans were packed thick in the sunken road, with the foremost line positioned behind the stone wall. Such a dense battle-line of gray and butternut soldiers behind such a formidable defensive position was ensured to deliver a heavy fire over the open fields before them.

From beginning to end, however, the frontal assault of the Irish Brigade was in reality little more than a forlorn hope. Like the fate of all other Union attackers who had hurled themselves against the formidable high ground of Marye's Heights, the attacking Celts were attempting to do the impossible.

All hell exploded in the faces of the Irish soldiers as they neared the menacing stone wall, when the first great volley was unleashed by hundreds of Rebels. Pvt. William McClelland, Eighty-eighth New York, wrote of the unbelievable slaughter, when "within thirty or forty yards of the rifle pits, where we met dreadful showers of bullets from three lines of the enemy, besides their enfilading fire [and] Our men were mowed down like grass before the scythe of the reaper [and] the men lay piled up in all directions."

With all other higher ranking regimental officers shot down, Capt. Patrick J. Condon now commanded what little was left of the hard-hit Sixty-third New York. Somehow escaping the hail of bullets, Color Sgt. Patrick Chambers, from County Mayo in northwest of Ireland, continued to encourage the Sixty-third New York forward by waving the colors back and forth amid the drifting palls of smoke.

Like the New York regiments, the 116th Pennsylvania was likewise shattered by the seemingly unceasing fire pouring from the stone wall. The entire color guard of the Keystone State regiment was cut down in short order. A badly wounded Color Sgt. William H. Terrill, with a broken leg and supporting himself on his one good knee, waved the flag in the faces of the Confederates one last time, before toppling over in a stream of bullets.

Major Mulholland went down with a wound early in the fight. He wrote: "The struggle was hopeless [as] The attacking line waved like corn in a hurricane . . . ." Sgt. Welsh described in his letter how, " . . . the storm of shot was then most galling and our ranks . . . . we had but a poor chance at the enemy who was sheltered in his rifel [sic] pits and entrenchments [and] I [have] seen some hot work at south mountain and antietam in maryland but they were not to be compared to this [as] old troops say that they never were under such a heavy fire before in any battle [and] every man that was near me in the right of the company [K] was either killed or wounded except one."

Indeed, despite no chance for success, the Celtic soldiers halted amid the bullet and shell-swept fields, gamely stood their ground, and fought back in spirited fashion. Meagher's men simply refused to retire. They now attempted to inflict some damage on their own upon their executioners, blasting away at the Confederates. Somehow, the surviving Irish soldiers hoped to salvage victory out of the jaws of defeat.

Before the blazing stone wall, the best efforts of the Irish soldiers were in vain. The slaughter was simply too great, and now ammunition was running low. To continue fighting any longer was folly. In truth, all chances of success had vanished as soon as the Irish Brigade's charge had lost its momentum. An Ohio soldier had watched in horror as the Irish Brigade was all but destroyed by the withering fire that seemed unceasing: "They reach a point within a stone's throw of the stone wall. No farther. They try to go beyond but are slaughtered. Nothing could advance farther and live." And Francis A. Walker described the no-win situation, saying: "Flesh and blood will not stand it any longer."

With many of his Massachusetts soldiers dead or dying around him, a carnage-numbed Colonel Byrnes could hardly believe his eyes. Above the tumult of battle, the horrified colonel yelled in horror to Capt. Patrick Joseph Condon, Sixty-third New York and who was born at Craves, County Limerick, in 1831, "The Brigade is gone."

Only after great sacrifice in life as in the struggle at the Bloody Lane of Antietam, the band of survivors of the Irish Brigade retired to escape the lethal fire that had consumed Meagher's command so swiftly and with such bloody efficiency. With twilight descending on the scene of carnage and with ammunition running low, small groups of Green Islanders withdrew through the drifting layers of smoke, stumbling over the bodies of their dead and wounded comrades.

Even though the Irish Brigade had withdrawn from the front upon receiving orders to do so, the heroics of the men in the ranks continued. With seemingly all of the soldiers of the 116th Pennsylvania regiment either dead or wounded, Lt. Francis T. Quinlan realized that the regimental colors had been left behind. So many color bearers had been killed or wounded that the regimental flag of the Pennsylvania regiment still lay among the fallen color guard.

Quinlan raced back to where the front of the Pennsylvania regiment had stood, now marked by the clusters of blue-uniformed bodies. Lieutenant Mulholland described Quinlan's the running of the gauntlet during his suicidal mission to reclaim the fallen flag: "A hundred [Rebels] fired at him, but quickly seizing the broken flag-staff threw himself on the ground, and then with the flag tightly clasped to his breast rolled back to where the command had halted, a noble deed, well done." Had Lieutenant Quinlan not possessed the presence of mind to remain on the ground and to then roll beyond the range of the barking Confederate rifles, he most certainly would have been either killed or seriously wounded. And if that had occurred, the Irish Brigade would have lost its first battle-flag of the war.

But the price had been paid in full by the Irish Brigade soldiers. Of the 1,200 Irish Brigade soldiers who charged Marye's Heights, 545 were either killed, wounded, captured, or missing, a loss of 45 percent for the Irish Brigade. The number of Irish soldiers who were killed was higher in proportion to the wounded than in any other battle, in part because many wounded left on the field froze to death in the night.

The Sixty-ninth New York lost 128 out of 238 men including sixteen of eighteen officers. The Eighty-eighth New York lost 4 officers and 13 enlisted men killed, while another 97 were wounded and 13 captured or missing, for a total of 127. One company of the Eighty-eighth New York came out of the holocaust with only seven soldiers, while another company was reduced to a single able-bodied man. The Sixty-third New York lost a total of 44 men, the lightest loss of any regiment of the Irish Brigade. Private McCarter wrote that the 116th Pennsylvania lost "27 killed, 84 wounded and 31 missing—total 142 men out of about 300 that went into action [. . .] The casualties were nearly 50 per cent of the whole command." The majority of the officers of this hard-fighting Pennsylvania regiment were either killed or wounded. Byrnes had led 426 soldiers of the Twenty-eighth Massachusetts, the largest regiment of the Irish Brigade into battle, and a total of 157 men became casualties.

Three of the five regimental commanders of the Irish Brigade were cut down including Col. Robert Nugent, Sixty-ninth New York, Maj. Joseph O'Neill, Sixty-third New York, and Colonel Heenan of the 116th Pennsylvania. O'Neill lost an arm to amputation, but survived to tell the story of Fredericksburg's horrors. The blood-soaked bodies of Maj. William Horgan and Adjutant John R. Young, of the Eighty-eighth New York, with the green sprigs of boxwood still in their hats, lay closest to the stone wall. Adjutant Young, "a truly noble man and officer" of much promise, would never again see his native King's County, Ireland.

With so many color bearers of the Sixty-ninth New York shot down, the regimental battle-flag failed to return from the body-littered killing ground before the stone wall. Later the next day, the blood-soaked banner was found stuffed inside the thick blue overcoat and wrapped around the body of the dead color sergeant. Even after the slaughter at Fredericksburg, the Irish Brigade could yet claim of having never lost a flag on the battlefield.

The holocaust of Fredericksburg all but destroyed the Irish Brigade, less than three months after it had lost more than 500 men at Antietam. The leading Irish newspaper of the nation, the *Irish-American*, complained that the young men and boys of the Irish Brigade had been used as little more than cannon fodder. But the Irish soldiers had lost none of their fighting spirit even in the face of disaster and staggering losses. "Beneath the smoke-cloud that rolled about Marye's Hill the Irish Brigade had ceased to exist," lamented Major Mulholland after the awful carnage.

Worst of all and unlike at Antietam, the slaughter at Fredericksburg had been for no gain, either political, tactical, or strategic. In the words of one angry Irish Brigade officer, "nothing of any good [was] obtained" at Fredericksburg.

An increasingly war-weary, but thankful Sgt. Welsh wrote to his wife, Margaret, in Charlestown, Massachusetts, on December 18, 1862: "thank God I came out of [the battle of Fredericksburg] safe [as] it was a fierce and bloody battle [and] our brigade got teribly [*sic*] cut up [and] it is so small now that it is not fit to go into any further action unless it is recruited up." And in an early 1863 letter, he penned with understatement that, "I do not want to ever get into such an afair [*sic*] as that again." Other Irish Brigade soldiers were equally disillusioned and heartsick over the slaughter at Fredericksburg. Capt. William J. Nagle, Eighty-eighth New York, wrote in a December 14, 1862 letter: "Irish blood and

A drawing of the ceremony held at St. Patrick's Cathedral in Lower Manhattan on January 16, 1863, for the fallen soldiers of the Irish Brigade, as it appeared in Frank Leslie's Illustrated Newspaper.

Irish bones cover that terrible field . . . We are slaughtered like sheep, and no result but defeat" once again.

The only gain won by the Irish Brigade at Fredericksburg was an even greater enhancement of its already lofty reputation across the North. But the price of glory was frightfully high. A member of General Meagher's staff, Capt. David Conyngham, wrote that "It will be a sad, sad Christmas [1862] by many an Irish hearthstone in New York, Pennsylvania, and Massachusetts." Indeed, hundreds of grieving relatives of Irish Brigade soldiers blessed the memory of their "lost" boys during Mass at small Catholic churches and big city cathedrals across the North.

After such a slaughter, the Irish Brigade was never the same. Not only had some of the best officers been killed or wounded, but also the finest men of the enlisted ranks were no more.

In an attempt to replenish the Irish Brigade's depleted ranks, an injured Meagher returned north to recruit from the sprawling Irish community of New York City, the largest concentration of Irish in the North.

On a frigid January 16, 1863 in New York City and while the cold winds blew off the Hudson River, an emotional tribute was held for the more than 1,500 Irish Brigade soldiers who had been lost in battles in Virginia and Maryland in less than two months. In the words of Father Corby: "While [General Meagher] was there [in New York City] a solemn Requiem Mass was celebrated for those of the brigade who fell during the campaign of 1862, and especially for those slaughtered at Fredericksburg. The Mass was celebrated in St. Patrick's Cathedral, and Father Ouellet, who had resigned from service, was the celebrant."

The Irish Brigade at Sunday Mass.

Among the traumatized Irish survivors, perhaps no one better understood this crisis than Father Corby. The influential Chaplain described the representative mood of the surviving band of Irishmen, who were now shrouded in the dark gloom of a very recent defeat and haunted by the loss of hundreds of comrades: "All of us were sad, very sad."

But as if to compensate for the tragedy, the Irish Brigade soldiers only became more devout. The horrors of battle and the repeated defeats suffered by the Army of the Potomac forged a more religious soldiery among the ever-thinning ranks of the Irish Brigade. The remaining Irishmen were indeed thankful to God that they had survived two of the war's greatest slaughters—Antietam and Fredericksburg.

Indicating the renewed amount of the religious devotion and spiritual activity in the Irish Brigade's encampment near Falmouth, Virginia, just north of Fredericksburg, Sergeant Welsh scribbled in a December 25, 1862, letter to his wife on a cold Christmas Day that, "I was at mass this morning . . . the 88th [New York] have an enclosure mad[e] in front of the chaplains' tent with cedar bushes and that forms the church with the little alter [sic] in the tent inside . . . God is good [as] he brought me safe out of this last battle and he can as easily bring me safe home to you if it is his holly [sic] will."

There was yet another factor that would soon add to the grief of the remaining Irish Brigade's soldiers.

Newspapers across the North were filled with tragic accounts of the suffering of the people of Ireland. As during the Great Famine of the 1840s, yet another food crisis swept across the Green Isle. The officers and men of the Irish Brigade donated $1200 for the relief of the Irish people on the other side of the Atlantic. Throughout the war years, the native homeland was never far from the minds of the Irish Brigade soldiers.

The new year of 1863 saw a new Irish Brigade. General Meagher's command of 1863 no longer resembled that crack fighting machine that had fought like few other combat units in 1862. The loss of more than 1,000 soldiers by bullets, bayonets, shells, and canister during the two great battles of Antietam and Fredericksburg left the Irish Brigade a mere shadow of its former self.

Besides attrition from the bloodiest battles of the eastern theater, the other great killer of Irish Brigade soldiers was the endless epidemic of disease that thinned the Celtic ranks without mercy. Unlike only a few hours of heavy fighting on a major battlefield, fatal diseases continued to strike down Irish Brigade's soldiers without a break. From the highest ranking officer to the lowest private, the best and brightest of the Irish Brigade were killed by the ravages of disease, which treated all ranks the same.

One of the most heartfelt losses sustained by the Irish Brigade by way of fatal illness was the death of young Lt. Temple Emmet, Eighty-eighth New York. Meagher wrote of the death of "Lieut. Temple Emmert [*sic*] whose death from typhoid fever the whole brigade affectionately and sincerely deplore . . . "

Lieutenant Emmet was the grand-nephew of famed Irish revolutionary, Robert Emmet, who led the 1803 revolt against the British. Robert Emmet had been hanged in September 1803 for inspiring the failed revolt. The young Dublin-born revolutionary became one of the most popular and enduring of all Irish nationalist heroes.

Out of a strong sense of duty, the brother of Lt. Temple Emmet, Richard Riker Emmet, felt the need to enlist in the Irish Brigade after his brother's death to fill the void. He served as a member of General Meagher's staff. Lt. Richard Emmet was fated to die not long after his enlistment, succumbing to "the same ailing as his brother."

While epidemics of disease almost always accounted for generally about double the number of fatalities in an average Union or Confederate brigade compared to battlefield losses, this was not the case in regard to the Irish Brigade. As a testament to both its hard fighting capabilities and its repeated employment in critical battlefield situations during some of

Drawings by Edwin Forbes of the 1863 St. Patrick's Day celebration by the Irish Brigade.

the most fiercely fought battles, the Irish Brigade lost two men on the battlefield for every one soldier who fell to disease.

The Irish Brigade's high losses had a detrimental effect on the home front. The disheartened wife of Sgt. Welsh, Margaret, wrote that the terrible losses suffered by the Irish Brigade had been largely in vain. She openly expressed her fears for the war's futility, lamenting the general apathy in the North in regard to the lengthy casualty lists of the Irish Brigade. Her soldier-husband was disturbed by the discouraging news. He wrote his wife: "You say there is not a word about the poor [Irish] felows [*sic*] who sacrifised [*sic*] their lives at fredericksburg no more then if they [had] never lived" at all.

The devastation of the Irish Brigade was so thorough that its tragic fate was even employed by Confederate secret agents in Ireland in the attempt to deter Irish immigrants from joining Union armies upon reaching America's shores. Confederate sympathizer Father John B. Bannon wrote one of his most effective pieces of propaganda in the form of handbills that were nailed up in 1864 on principal buildings and churches near major emigrant departure points at the major ports of Ireland, such as Galway. These handbills emphasized the brutal lesson of the Irish Brigade's slaughter at Fredericksburg for all young Irish immigrants who contemplated wearing a blue uniform in America.

Father Bannon, Irish-born himself, warned Irish immigrants, especially Catholics, of their eventual tragic fate when "He becomes a soldier [and] In 48 hours he is landed in the Swamps of the Carolinas, or on the Sand Bars of

Union Gen. Joseph Hooker, commander of the Army of the Potomac.

Charleston [and] There to imbrue his hands in THE BLOOD OF HIS COUNTRYMEN [of the South], and fight for a People [Northerners and Protestants] that has the greatest antipathy to his birth and creed. Let Irishmen remember the fate of MEAGHER'S Brigade, on the bloody field of Fredericksburg, 5,000 strong! . . . Some of the New York [City] Papers [were] stating that they could afford to lose a few thousand of the scum of the Irish."

Peter Welsh's burning personal ambition was fulfilled during the festive celebration on St. Patrick's Day, 1863 when he was made the color sergeant of the Twenty-eighth Massachusetts. With pride, Color Sgt. Welsh wrote to his wife that, "I must tell you now that I have the honor of carrying the green flag." When handed the green flag of Ireland decorated with the wreath of shamrocks, Irish harp, and the Gaelic war-motto of "Clear the Way," the deeply-religious Color Sgt. Welsh swore to "carry it as long as God gives me strength." Like the men in the ranks, Color Sgt. Welsh felt deep reverence for this silk banner "on account of it being the green flag of old Irland [*sic*]."

For the young Irish Brigade soldiers, war against the Confederacy continued to be viewed as a moral and righteous crusade. These Celts were committed to the struggle to preserve the United States, which served as the shining beacon of hope and place of refuge for the oppressed people of Ireland for generations.

In part because of the ceaseless thinning of its ranks during the bloody battles of 1862, the Irish Brigade would be spared in the next great clash of arms in Virginia between the Army of the Potomac and the Army of Northern Virginia, when the spring campaign of 1863 opened. Gen. Joseph Hooker, Burnside's replacement as commander of the Army of the Potomac, began offensive operations after extensive preparations for a new spring campaign in Virginia. Hooker believed that by out-flanking the Confederates he could win an easy victory that might decide the war's outcome.

But it was Hooker and not Lee who was suddenly out-flanked in the dense springtime forests of the Rapidan and Rappahannock River country of Virginia. In one of the most famous flank marches of the war, "Stonewall" Jackson shifted his corps west and parallel to the Union army without detection. Displaying characteristic aggressiveness, he then turned eastward and struck hard at the unprepared Yankee right wing. Catching the Federals by surprise, Jackson's troops slammed into Hooker's exposed right flank, held by the ill-fated Eleventh Corps, in the dark woodlands of Chancellorsville on the south side of the Rapidan River on the morning of May 2, 1863.

At the battle of Chancellorsville, the Irish Brigade played a relatively minor role. The brigade remained in position while most combat occurred on the right flank of Hooker's Army. Nevertheless, morale was high, and the Irishmen were eager for action.

On May 3, the second day of the battle of Chancellorsville, the Irish Brigade advanced to the front to reinforce the heavily-pressured lines. The Irish troops deployed in a long battle-line before the advancing Rebels, who were intoxicated with their success. Here, the Irishmen in blue came under a severe artillery fire. Casualties rose when shells exploded in the packed ranks of the Irish troops.

Lt. Col. Richard C. Bentley, Sixty-third New York, was wounded by an exploding shell. An iron shell fragment hit him in the head, leaving him bloody and dizzy. As he wrote later in a letter to his father: "I received a piece of shell, burst in the air, on the head, which passed through the centre of the top of my hat, grazing my head, without cutting out the side, through the rim, and tore through my coat, vest and shirt, at the back of my left shoulder [but] I remained in command nearly an hour before I felt any effect, save a slight shock [soon however] I sat down and keeled over and was taken to the rear." Bentley was fortunate to survive the nasty wound. Despite playing a relatively minor role at Chancellorsville, the Irish Brigade suffered more than 100 casualties, the result of the deadly rain of falling shells.

Chancellorsville was yet another crushing defeat for the Army of the Potomac. The tactical mastery of the dynamic leadership team of Lee and Jackson, was once again simply too much for Hooker and the Army of the Potomac to overcome. Yet another massive Union effort to capture Richmond ended in the defeat amid the bloody woodlands of Chancellorsville. Only around 400 Irish soldiers were left in the ranks of Meagher's Brigade after Chancellorsville.

Defeat at Chancellorsville was yet another blow to the Irish Brigade troops. Additional Celtic soldiers had been lost for no gain. An increasingly disillusioned Color Sgt. Welsh described in a letter: "we had another grand scadadle [*sic*]

[and] by some mismanagement our left was broken [by Stonewall Jackson's flank attack] and our army [was] compelled to fall back . . . we did not have to do any fiting [sic] but the shelling was terific [sic]."

But since the Irish Brigade had seen relatively little fighting at Chancellorsville, some Irish ceased to believe that they were only being used by the Lincoln government and army leadership as cannon fodder. In part to explain the disproportionate losses of the Irish Brigade, the opinion had developed that because they were Irish and Catholics, the Irish were expendable to the Protestant government and nation. According to this conspiratorial theory, the army and government could willingly sacrifice a high number of Irish soldiers without having to suffer the negative political and domestic repercussions from an immigrant population representing the lowest rung of the social ladder and with relatively little political clout. Republican leaders, both military and civilian, seemingly had no qualms about hurling large numbers of these staunch Irish Democrats and devout Catholics to their deaths. And Meagher was a popular Democrat who enjoyed little support in the Republican Administration of President Lincoln.

However, many, including General Meagher, did not believe that the Irish Brigade was being deliberately sacrificed. To be sure, the Irish Brigade had been thoroughly savaged, and no one was angrier about that ugly reality than Meagher. The general repeatedly requested replacements for the Irish Brigade, but none were forthcoming. In addition, he requested that his three New York regiments be allowed to return to New York City to recruit to fill their depleted ranks, but his request was denied. Consequently, it seemed as if the War Department in Washington, D.C. was more than willing to allow the Irish Brigade to be used up and wither away through brutal attrition until relatively little remained of a once magnificent combat unit.

With the once mighty Irish Brigade now reduced to less than 400 soldiers, a war-weary Meagher, no longer the idealistic Young Irelander, submitted his resignation because "the Irish Brigade no longer exists." Meagher had powerful political opponents in the Republican government, who made sure that his resignation was accepted without hesitation. Dominated by politics and bitter in-fighting, the Army of the Potomac waged its own internal political wars, as fiercely as it fought Lee's Army. Meagher's resignation became official on May 13. If Meagher's resignation had been intended as a measure to force quick concessions for the Irish Brigade's benefit, then that strategy backfired.

During an emotional farewell to the Irish Brigade soldiers, Meagher explained that he retired because "the Irish Brigade no longer" existed. He offered "an affectionate farewell [but] I cannot do so, however, without leaving on record the assurance of the happiness, the gratitude and pride with which I revert to the first days of the Irish Brigade, when it struggled in its infancy and was sustained alone by its native strength and instincts; and retrace from the field, where it first displayed its brilliant gallantry, all the efforts, all the hardships, all the privations, all the sacrifices which have made its history, brief though it be, sacred and inestimable [and now] I have been preserved to bring comfort to those who have lost fathers, husbands, and brothers in the soldiers who have fallen for a noble government under the green flag . . . The graves of many hundreds of brave and devoted soldiers, who went to death with all the radiance and enthusiasm of the noblest chivalry, are so many guarantees and pledges that, as long as there remains one officer or soldier of the Irish Brigade, so long shall there be found for him, for his family and little ones, if any there be, a devoted friend in Thomas Francis Meagher."

Drawn up in a square with their beloved general in the formation's center, the Irish soldiers unleashed a chorus of cheers in response to Meagher's address. Then, in an emotional act that was unusual for a brigade commander, Meagher went to great lengths to say personal goodbyes to both men and officers. With a warm sincerity and reflecting the deep feelings that the Irish soldiers held for him, General Meagher said good-bye to nearly every soldier in his command. And the general personally shook hands with as many Irish Brigade members as possible. Tears flowed freely between the general and his men during the emotional farewell.

Then, the heart and soul of the Irish Brigade departed the legendary unit that he had led with typical Irish aggressiveness on May 19. General Meagher left Col. Patrick Kelly in charge of what little remained of the Irish Brigade. The physically imposing, dark-featured Colonel Kelly had come a long way from the more innocent days when he had marched as a lowly private in the ranks of the Sixty-ninth New York State Militia, and when the war was yet a romantic adventure for the vast majority of young Irishmen from New York City. But while Meagher was now gone, the lofty reputation of the Irish Brigade was destined to grow in future campaigns.

Meagher's departure temporarily affected the morale of the Irish Brigade, but not its fighting spirit. Capt. William J. Nagle, Eighty-eighth New York wrote in a letter to his father: "The resignation of our beloved chief, Gen. Meagher, has been accepted, and with him go our hearts, our hopes and our inspiration." The founder and inspirational leader of the Irish Brigade departed just before his unit descended into the surreal carnage of the most climactic battle of the Civil War at a little town in Pennsylvania—Gettysburg.

CHAPTER 5

The Wheatfield at Gettysburg

Despite the horrendous losses of 1862, the Irish Brigade was destined to rise to the next great challenge of Gettysburg, resurrecting the hard-fighting performances demonstrated at Antietam and Fredericksburg. This feat would be no small achievement. Indeed, from the summer of 1862 to December 13, 1862 at Fredericksburg, the Irish Brigade had suffered more than 1,500 casualties. Few, if any, brigades on either side had suffered so severely in such a short time. And few units could have survived such a severe decimation of its ranks without a thorough erosion of their combat capabilities. But this was not the case with the Irish Brigade.

In another attempt to fulfill the dream of winning decisive victory north of the Potomac that had been denied him during the Maryland Campaign, General Lee led the Army of Northern Virginia northward in its second invasion of the North in the early summer of 1863. The soldiers of the much reduced Irish Brigade and the rest of the Army of the

Union Gen. John Curtis Caldwell, commander of the First Division, Second Corps, Army of the Potomac.

Potomac pushed north along the dusty roads that led to the small town in southeastern Pennsylvania, Gettysburg.

By this time, the 116th Pennsylvania had been reduced to a weak battalion of only four companies, a total of 66 soldiers, under the command of Major Mulholland. The Pennsylvania regiment was now the smallest unit of the Irish Brigade. But the other regiments of the Irish Brigade, now part of Gen. John C. Caldwell's First Division, Second Corps, were nearly as reduced in strength as the 116th Pennsylvania.

However, around 530 soldiers remained in the Irish Brigade ranks, and they were destined to play a key role in the upcoming climactic clash at Gettysburg. As always, the fighting spirit of the Irish Brigade remained high, especially when it came to defending northern territory. In this sense, the performance of the Irish at Gettysburg would be comparable to that of Antietam, a battlefield performance far beyond their numbers.

The Irishmen in blue, though weary from the long march to Gettysburg through the searing summer heat, were still highly motivated. As during the Maryland Campaign, they were determined to drive the Confederates out of the North at any cost. Naturally, this motivation was highest among the soldiers of the 116th Pennsylvania. For the first time, the Pennsylvania troops would be defending home soil. For the Irish of the 116th Pennsylvania, this war had suddenly become a much more personal affair.

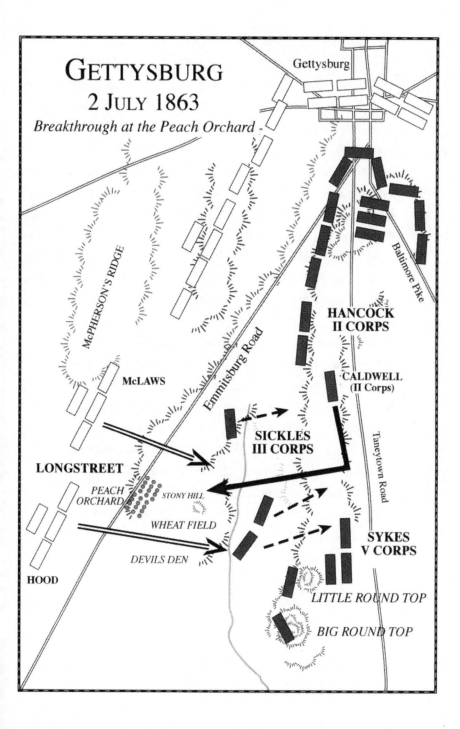

GETTYSBURG
2 JULY 1863
Breakthrough at the Peach Orchard

Gettysburg

McPHERSON'S RIDGE

Emmitsburg Road

Baltimore Pike

HANCOCK
II CORPS

McLAWS

CALDWELL
(II Corps)

SICKLES
III CORPS

Taneytown Road

LONGSTREET

PEACH
ORCHARD

STONY HILL

WHEAT FIELD

DEVILS DEN

SYKES
V CORPS

HOOD

LITTLE ROUND TOP

BIG ROUND TOP

Though Meagher was no longer leading the Irish Brigade, the Celtic warriors could not have had by a better commanding officer than Col. Patrick Kelly. Kelly had migrated to America in 1850, after witnessing the Great Famine's horrors that had swept Ireland. Kelly had come a long way from the life as a lowly tenant farmer in County Galway.

Kelly was a veteran of First Manassas, having fought in the ranks of the Sixty-ninth New York State Militia. When the Irish Brigade was organized, Kelly became the lieutenant colonel of the Eighty-eighth New York, but he soon succeeded to command of this fine regiment from New York City. He led this Empire State regiment into the fray at Fair Oaks and at Antietam. By this time, no officer in the Irish Brigade was more respected than Colonel Kelly.

Kelly was fortunate to have a number of trusty top lieutenants to assist him during the Pennsylvania Campaign. As usual and as demonstrated on the fields of Fredericksburg and Chancellorsville, Colonel Byrnes, the old army regular who now commanded the Twenty-eighth Massachusetts, could be thoroughly relied upon. The New England command was the largest regiment of the Irish Brigade by this time, even though it contained a mere 224 soldiers. Clearly, the Irish Brigade was a far different command from that lethal fighting machine that had charged into the inferno of Fredericksburg.

Born on the Hudson River in Albany, New York, and lately a successful shipping merchant at the state capital, thirty-year-old Lt. Col. Richard Charles Bentley now led the 75 soldiers of the Sixty-third New York. Bentley had only recently recovered from a Chancellorsville wound. Additionally,

Bentley had also been wounded in the attack on the "Bloody Lane" at Antietam. But neither wound had diminished Bentley's determination to fight to the bitter end.

An equally dependable and capable officer, Capt. Richard Moroney, now commanded the Sixty-ninth New York. Like Bentley, Moroney was a native New Yorker. Despite his relatively low rank for a regimental commander, Captain Moroney possessed plenty of solid experience that made him an excellent leader. He had served in the militia of New York City, and had fought in the Mexican-American War. In addition, Moroney had been commended for valor at Antietam. Moroney was described as not only a good officer, but also "witty, genial, and a universal favorite." Captain Moroney now commanded 75 men of the Sixty-ninth New York.

Capt. Denis Francis Burke, only 22, was a former New York City merchant who now led what little remained of the Eighty-eighth New York, some 90 soldiers. He was born in County Cork in the sunny south of Ireland. He felt great pride in his Celtic origin and Gaelic culture. Burke was shot in the left arm at Fredericksburg, and was then wounded in the head by a shell fragment at Chancellorsville, but had recovered sufficiently to head the depleted regiment.

Commanding the Keystone Staters of the 116th Pennsylvania, Maj. St. Clair Mulholland had been born in County Antrim in northeast Ireland. Before the war, this versatile Ulsterman had preferred artistic beauty and graceful proportion to thoughts of a military life. In those days of innocence before the insanity of civil war, Mulholland had found fulfillment as a promising painter in Philadelphia.

Union Gen. George Gordon Meade, who replaced Gen. Joseph Hooker as commander of the Army of the Potomac just days before the Battle of Gettysburg.

With high hopes and with .69 caliber muskets on shoulders, the jaunty Irishmen slogged along the dusty Taneytown Road during the rapid-paced march to join the army attempting to make a defensive stand at Gettysburg. After Lee's forces initiated contact on July 1 the Army of the Potomac attempted to concentrate as rapidly as possible at Gettysburg. Late in the afternoon, the weary Irish Brigade soldiers came to a halt near Cemetery Ridge, just east and southeast of the agricultural community.

The Emerald Islanders fell into line with the rest of the army. Here, they took a defensive position along a lengthy elevation known as Cemetery Ridge, where Gen. George Meade, who had replaced Hooker, hoped to concentrate his wide-ranging units before it was too late. Along the high ground of Cemetery Ridge, Meade had wisely decided to make his defensive stand. In what was essentially a Malvern Hill-like repeat, he offered the ever-aggressive Lee an opportunity to strike a blow and to expend his manpower on July 2.

And that powerful blow from the Army of Northern Virginia was unleashed in the late afternoon on the second day of the battle of Gettysburg. Lee hurled the veteran divisions of Gen. James Longstreet's Corps forward in an attack en echelon from the parallel ridge, Seminary Ridge, in an attempt to roll up the left flank of the Army of the Potomac. Lee's desperate bid to win the war now rested upon one throw of the dice on July 2. He hoped to capitalize on his success on July 1, when his elated Rebel troops had beaten and driven the Union army's advance elements through the small town of Gettysburg.

Before the Irish Brigade troops entered yet another bloody battle, Father Corby played his most dramatic part in the unit's history. Chaplain Corby was now not only thinking about saving the souls of so many young Irishmen and other nearby soldiers, both Catholic and Protestant. He knew that some of these young men and boys were about to meet their Maker on fateful July 2. After obtaining the approval of Colonel Kelly, who knew the importance of such an inspirational gesture on

Confederate Gen. James Longstreet.

the eve of entering yet another great battle, the chaplain stood atop a rocky outcropping, so that the Irish Brigade soldiers could see and hear him above the roar of battle, which was growing ever-higher to the west.

Maintaining his usual quiet dignity under fire, Chaplain Corby began to bestow a general absolution on hundreds of kneeing Irish soldiers, who solemnly bowed heads and prayed just before entering the biggest battle of their lives. An Irish Brigade officer wrote how: "the brigade stood in a column of regiments, close in mass," while Father Corby "remind[ed] them of the high and sacred nature of their trust as solders . . . Then, stretching his right hand toward the brigade [he] pronounced the [Latin] words of absolution. The service was more than impressive, it was awe-inspiring."

With green banners and national colors flapping in the late afternoon sunshine, the Irish pushed swiftly south toward Little Round Top at the southern end of the Union battle-line.

Then, all of a sudden, the Irish brigade and the other three brigades of General Caldwell's Division were ordered to turn west to gain possession of the Wheat Field, just northwest of Little Round Top and southeast of the Peach Orchard. The Confederates of Longstreet's Corps had smashed through Gen. Dan Sickles's Third Corps and captured the Peach Orchard. The breakthrough at the vulnerable Peach Orchard salient opened the way for thousands of victorious Southerners to charge unimpeded east toward Cemetery Ridge. The Rebel tide pouring eastward through the Wheat Field had to be stemmed at all costs, or Lee would finally have won his long-sought decisive victory on northern soil.

The surging ranks of the Irish Brigade soon fell under a heavy artillery fire from Col. Edward Alexander's guns positioned on the high ground of the Peach Orchard amid the broken debris of the Third Corps.

On the run, the cheering Irish soldiers entered the waving stalks of the northern part of the Wheat Field. A rain of Rebel shells exploded amid the onrushing ranks of the Irishmen, who continued to pour forward with fixed bayonets. Bentley fell at the head of his regiment. He dropped into the wheat with a mangled leg. Nevertheless, the Irish of the Sixty-third New York continued onward through the waist-high wheat and searing heat of summer.

At the edge of the Wheat Field, the primary bone of contention was the little rocky eminence in the woods known as Stony Hill. Here, more than 2,000 veteran South Carolina soldiers of Kershaw's tough brigade advanced. General Kershaw's brigade charged below, or south of, the Peach Orchard, to occupy the high ground of Stony Hill.

The Rebels were so close that the spunky Irish shouted curses and jeers at them. Making a defensive stand, the Carolinians now possessed the tactical advantage, blasting away from the good cover of the crest of Stony Hill, and from behind rocks, trees, and boulders.

Here the Irish reaped a measure of revenge for the slaughter at Fredericksburg. Along with Georgia troops, these veteran South Carolina soldiers under Kershaw had defended the stone wall and sunken road of Marye's Heights to cut the Irish Brigade to pieces. Leading the Pennsylvania troops, Major Mulholland never forgot the moment when: "As we approached the crest of the rugged [stony] hill, from behind the huge boulders that were everywhere scattered around them, the men of Longstreet's corps rose up and poured into our ranks a most destructive fire. The sudden meeting astonished us, the lines not more than thirty feet apart . . . . "

The close-range blasts of "buck and ball" ammunition from the Irish smoothbore muskets was more deadly than the Confederate rifles, spraying a lead shot that cut down a good many South Carolina soldiers. While the Rebels possessed the tactical advantage of the high ground, the Irish possessed the technical advantage of "buck and ball."

Throughout the bitter struggle, the emerald green flags of Ireland led the way through the snarled trees and the sulfurous clouds of smoke and up the rocky eastern slope of the Stony Hill. Poised along the rocky crest, South Carolina soldiers blasted away in a futile attempt to stop the steam-rolling Celtic attack.

The Confederate dead awaiting burial at Rose Woods, July 5, 1863.

No longer believing that they could repeat their Fredericksburg success on this bloody afternoon, the South Carolina troops defending the high ground were swept away by the raging Irish tide that poured through the rocks and trees to crash over the summit of Stony Hill. The battered remains of two South Carolina regiments, the Third and Seventh South Carolina, fell back to the relative safety of the woods and fields of the John Rose farm on the west side of Stony Hill. Soon the emerald flags waived from the crest of the body-littered hill. But this success in overwhelming the South Carolina Rebels and capturing the high ground was not enough to satisfy Irish ambitions. By this time, the fighting blood of the Irishmen was up. Sensing that their victory could be additionally exploited, the Irish soldiers continued to advance with cheers. Colonel Kelly's soldiers now poured down through the rocks and trees along the west slope of Stony Hill. Kelly then deployed his troops in a defensive line on good terrain on the Rose farm.

In overall tactical terms, the success of the Irish Brigade was impressive. Kelly's Celtic troops had first swept the Wheat Field clean of Confederates, overwhelmed the defenses of Stony Hill, and then had taken yet more ground farther beyond the rocky elevation. Most important, the Irish Brigade had bought precious time for additional Union troops to be sent forward to reinforce and eventually restore the battered left of the Army of the Potomac.

But the success achieved by the Irish in overrunning Stony Hill lasted for only a short time. The advanced position of the Irish soldiers was quickly compromised when Gen. William Wofford's Georgians advanced eastward to support Kershaw's left. The attacking veterans from the Peach State now threatened the right flank of Caldwell's Division. Color Sergeant Welsh wrote that the Rebels "threw a heavy force against the brigade on the right of ours, driving in our flank [and] by this we were compeled [*sic*] to fall back. . . ."

Caldwell ordered his hard-hit division, which was nearly surrounded, to retire before it was too late. The Irish survivors of the fight for Stony Hill now had to run a deadly gauntlet of fire to escape the attacking Rebels. Major

Mulholland wrote how "this [was the] alley of death" for the Irish Brigade. Colonel Kelly later related "We have encountered a most terrific fire, and narrowly escaped being captured."

After barely escaping the raging tide of victorious Rebels and the tactical trap that the Wheat Field had suddenly become, the battered Irish Brigade and Caldwell's Division retired east toward Cemetery Ridge and to a rallying point along the Taneytown Road. Soon the surviving Irishmen took up their original defensive position on Cemetery Ridge, along with the rest of Caldwell's division. Here, the Irish survivors, exhausted and powder-stained, spent the night of July 2.

The next day, July 3, Lee unleashed his last and most desperate attempt to break the powerful Union defensive line along the commanding high ground of Cemetery Ridge. As Meade envisioned, the massive frontal assaults against formidable Cemetery Ridge resulted in the folly of unleashing ill-fated "Pickett's Charge," that ended in defeat. During the Confederate assault, the Irishmen watched from behind a sturdy breastwork of rock and fence rails along Cemetery Ridge. The sons of Erin endured a heavy bombardment in the hours before Lee's final bid to salvage a decisive success. But the Emerald Islanders were spared harder fighting on July 3.

As at Antietam and Fredericksburg, the Irish Brigade suffered heavy casualties on July 2, which witnessed the heaviest fighting during the three days of combat at Gettysburg. The Irish Brigade had lost almost another 40 percent of its strength, with more than two hundred soldiers killed, wounded, or captured. Of the 530 soldiers upon whom Father Corby had bestowed absolution along Cemetery Ridge, a total of

202 were killed, wounded, or captured in the vicious struggle at Stony Hill and the Wheat Field.

In a letter to his wife, Peter Welsh wrote with understatement how the Irish Brigade once again "lost heavely [*sic*]
[as] the killed[,] wounded and missing of our little regiment
is over a hundred. Out of the five regiments that form this
brigade there is but men enough here present to make three
full companys [*sic*]." The Twenty-eighth Massachusetts was
the largest regiment of the Irish Brigade at Gettysburg, and
suffered the most grievous losses. Of the total of 224
Massachusetts Irishmen entered the battle, more than 100
were lost at Gettysburg.

But unlike at Fredericksburg, the severe losses suffered
by the Irish Brigade had not been in vain. Gettysburg was the
high water mark of the Confederacy. General Lee and his
Army of Northern Virginia had lost their bid to win decisive
victory north of the Potomac. As never before, the fortunes
of war had turned against the Confederacy.

CHAPTER 6

The Road to Appomattox Court House

The Irish Brigade next saw action in the early fall of 1863. A soldier of the Eighty-eighth New York described the Irish Brigade's role at the battle of Bristoe Station, Virginia: "On the 14th [of October, 1863] we were shelled at breakfast by the advance of the enemy, fought six hours in retreat, capturing the first battery by a coup de main, encountered them ten miles further on at Bristoe Station, fought, with two divisions, the whole of A.P. Hill's corps, held our position till after midnight, Irish Brigade last, alone and unsupported, till the others were safe at a distance, then a double-quick for twelve miles, a march of 76 miles in 56 hours, fighting two severe engagements in one day, and having to guard the entire baggage and reserve artillery of the army. This is unprecedented in the annals of war. We captured two colors, five guns and four hundred and fifty prisoners, and lost nothing."

The Mine Run campaign of November 1863, the winter of 1863-1864 was a time of recuperation for the soldiers of

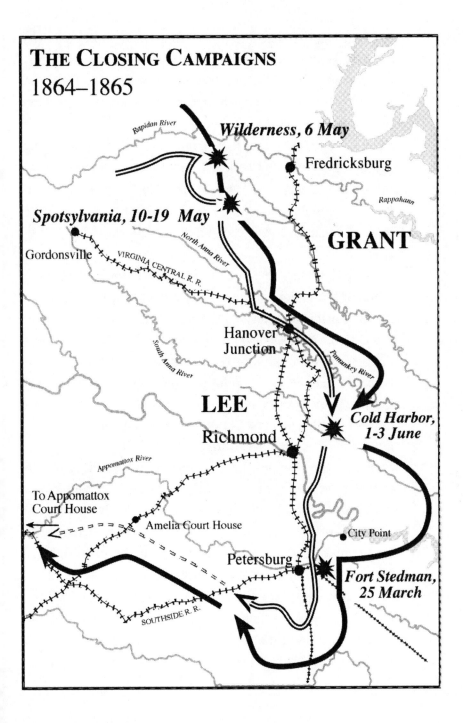

THE CLOSING CAMPAIGNS 1864–1865

Rapidan River

Wilderness, 6 May

Fredricksburg

Rappahann

GRANT

Spotsylvania, 10-19 May

Gordonsville

VIRGINIA CENTRAL R. R.

North Anna River

South Anna River

Hanover Junction

Pamunkey River

LEE

Richmond

Cold Harbor, 1-3 June

Appomattox River

To Appomattox Court House

Amelia Court House

City Point

Petersburg

Fort Stedman, 25 March

SOUTHSIDE R. R.

Kelly's brigade. By the late fall of 1863, the Irish Brigade was established in winter quarters north of the Rapidan River. It was a time to replenish the thinned ranks. In early 1864, the relatively few surviving Irish Brigade members were granted thirty-day furloughs for reenlisting to serve for the war's duration. The veterans returned home for thirty days, visiting families that they had believed they would never see again. In addition, recruiters were dispatched to New York City, Boston, and Philadelphia to recruit volunteers to fill the thinned ranks of the five diminutive regiments of the Irish Brigade.

Despite the vigorous recruiting efforts in the Irish communities of the major northeastern cities, the Irish Brigade in its 1862 prime was never fully reconstituted to regain its old form. This was not only due to the lack of willing manpower but also because the new recruits were no longer the idealistic Irish immigrants who had volunteered to form the Irish Brigade in the heady days of 1861. A war-weariness and even anti-war feeling had crept into the northern populace, including the Irish community by this time.

Thereafter, in consequence, the Irish Brigade gradually lost more of its distinctive Irish character, and hence its overall high quality. From now on, the Irish Brigade would perform more like other good combat brigades of the Army of the Potomac, rather than the elite fighting machine of Antietam and Fredericksburg. In January, 1864, an emotional toast by one Irish Brigade officer, which was more a lament than a tribute, indicated the bitter and haunting reality that could no longer be denied: "The Irish Brigade [or] what there is left of it."

The unit continued to serve as only a shadow of its former self.

A journalist of the Irish-American newspaper of Boston, *The Pilot*, bemoaned the tragedy of the Irish Brigade's fate by this time: "Our fighters are dead" and have been left lying in shallow graves and burial trenches across three states, Virginia, Maryland, and Pennsylvania. Color Sergeant Welsh, becoming more embittered over the Irish Brigade's diminished ranks, wrote perhaps the saddest lament to his wife: "God help the Irish."

For such reasons, recruitment for the Irish Brigade was painfully slow. In fact, enthusiastic volunteering to serve for three years in the most brutal conflict in American history to date was understandably low across the North because of war-weariness. In addition, General Meagher was now gone. The Young Irelander of 1848 was no longer the magnet that attracted young Irishmen to the Irish Brigade as in 1861. While many veterans reenlisted for the war, the composition and character of the Irish Brigade evolved into a new unit hardly recognizable from the zenith of its glory days of 1862.

By the time of the celebration of St. Patrick's Day on March 17, 1864, around 80 percent of the Irish Brigade's strength consisted of new recruits. In overall demographic terms, these newcomers were much less Irish, in both blood and outlook, than at any previous time. Many men had been conscripted by the draft, which was especially unpopular with the Irish. Consequently, much time in early 1864 was devoted to instructing and drilling these new soldiers in the hope of reaching the Irish Brigade's high standards of discipline and performance. Because of the absence of so many highly-moti-

Col. Thomas Alfred Smyth, commander of the Irish Brigade.

vated veterans, especially among the decimated officer corps, the Irish Brigade would never repeat its combat performances of the past in the days ahead. But that fact did not mean that the high attrition rate among the Irish Brigade soldiers would not continue unabated in the fighting that lay ahead.

Thanks to a string of impressive victories across the western theater, especially in capturing Vicksburg, Mississippi, on July 4, 1863 and then Chattanooga, Tennessee, later in the year, Gen. Ulysses S. Grant was given overall command of the Union forces, including the Army of the Potomac. He formulated his spring 1864 campaign to crush Lee and the Army of Northern Virginia by directing a massive offensive toward the Army of the Potomac's longtime goal of Richmond. In early May, 1864, Grant prepared to hurl his forces south across the Rapidan River in a great offensive drive.

Col. Thomas Alfred Smyth, a native of Fermoy, County Cork who had migrated to the United States in 1854, now commanded the Irish Brigade. Smyth had been one of filibusters under William Walker in Nicaragua before the Civil War and before settling down as a coach maker in Wilmington, Delaware. He had already demonstrated considerable leadership ability in leading the First Delaware Volunteer Infantry. After his March 1864 appointment to command the Irish Brigade, Colonel Smyth became "a great favorite" of the men in the ranks. A tough disciplinarian who left his positive impact on the Irish Brigade, Smyth was the last Union general killed in battle, falling only two days before Lee's surrender in April 1865.

The main theater of operations in the spring campaign of 1864 was once again the rolling, heavily-forested countryside of central Virginia. The North marshaled its vast resources and manpower for yet another determined drive to capture the Confederacy's capital to end the war. Supremely confident from his western successes that made him Lincoln's best general, Grant was determined to win the war before the year's end.

With its ranks replenished to a strength of more than 2,000 soldiers, the Irish Brigade crossed the Rapidan River with Grant's army. The Green Islanders embarked upon a fresh campaign under a new commander of considerable strategic and tactical ability. But this campaign in the depths of Virginia was destined to be far different from all others.

In the sweltering Virginia forests of early May, the Army of the Potomac and the Army of Northern Virginia clashed head on just south of the Rapidan. Here, along with Grant's massive army of more than 100,000 troops, the Irish Brigade was engaged in the bitter fighting that became known as the Battle of the Wilderness.

Along the Brock Road that cut through the thick woodlands of second growth pine, hickory, and oak west of Fredericksburg and south of the Wilderness Tavern, the Irish soldiers smashed into Lee's troops on May 5. The confused fighting of the Wilderness degenerated into a disconnected jumble of small unit actions rather than a traditional clash of opposing armies. The fighting was disorganized and confused because of the gullied and rough terrain, thick foliage, and almost impenetrable forests of underbrush, vines, and creepers that more looked like jungle than the typical hardwood forests.

Lt. Col. George Washington Cartwright, commanding the Twenty-eighth Massachusetts, fell with a bad wound to the left shoulder. Additional Irish soldiers who demonstrated valor in the Wilderness served in the ranks of the Massachusetts regiment. A "morocco dresser" from Lynn, Massachusetts, Capt. James A. McIntyre dashed before the main line to assist a wounded Irish skirmisher to safety amid a hail of bullets, but was shot down and killed. Perhaps the most significant loss suffered by the Irish Brigade in the Wilderness on May 5 was the "unassuming" Maj. Thomas Touhy of County Claire, Ireland. He fell when a bullet whistled through the right lung, a wound which soon proved fatal to this officer of promise.

The savage fighting in the Wilderness on May 5 was only the opening of the conflict south of the Rapidan. On the sweltering hot afternoon of May 6, General Hancock's Second Corps attacked once again. But Lee's forces soon gained the upper hand. Lee hurled more units of Longstreet's Corps into the fray, gaining the initiative. Along with the rest of Hancock's divisions of the Second Corps, the Irish Brigade was attacked by a seemingly endless number of howling Confederates amid tangled forests and rough terrain cut by creeks and gullies. Fortunately, the Emerald Islanders held a fine defensive position. Behind a solid log breastwork along the dusty Brock Road that cut through the dark woodlands like a red clay ribbon, the Green Islanders prepared to meet the surging Rebel tide. When the Confederates struck, the

Wounded from the Battle of the Wilderness.

Irish Brigade soldiers were ready and waiting. In his diary, Cpl. Samuel Clear, 116th Pennsylvania, described the Rebel assault: "On they came with a woman like scream [and] then we let them have the buck and Ball from behind the old logs and brush."

Grant's forces suffered almost 18,000 casualties in the Wilderness, but, instead of the customary withdrawal, Grant decided to retain the all-important initiative. He knew that this aggressive strategy was necessary to win this war once and for all. Consequently, he ordered his battered Army of the Potomac forward instead of withdrawing to the north side of the Rapidan River, as so many other previous commanders of the Army of the Potomac would have done.

The bloody two-day battle of the Wilderness in early May was not another Chancellorsville as had been feared by the Irish in the ranks. Instead, the continued offensive effort revealed the firm commitment by Grant to continue pushing toward Richmond, while continuing to punish the Army of Northern Virginia in a determined bid to end the war. Most significant of all, Grant's strategy was focused on destroying the Army of Northern Virginia rather than simply capturing Richmond—a new revelation that promised decisive victory.

The Union general next targeted the key crossroads at Spotsylvania Court House, which was located southeast of the Wilderness and a dozen miles closer to Richmond, as his next objective. Grant embarked upon a strategy of attempting to outflank Lee's army by sliding leftward, part of the strategic plan of applying constant pressure upon the Army of Northern Virginia—the key to success in a war of attrition. Both armies raced for the vital crossroads at Spotsylvania, and the little dirt roads that led to Richmond which had suddenly become strategically important. Alerted to the tenacious quality of the opposing commanding general, the Army of Northern Virginia hastened toward Spotsylvania Court House.

Lee reacted quickly to Grant's movement and won the race to secure the crossroads at Spotsylvania Court House. There, the hardened veterans of Lee's army created a masterful defensive network in preparation for meeting the Army of the Potomac.

Consequently, when Grant found the way to Spotsylvania Court House blocked by the Army of Northern Virginia, he ordered a frontal attack. Before dawn in the rainy darkness of May 12, the Irish Brigade assaulted a strong defensive salient known as the "Mule Shoe." Two divisions of General Hancock's Second Corps struck the extended apex of the salient held by Gen. Richard S. Ewell's Corps.

After picking their way through a thick abatis of felled trees, the attackers of the Second Corps, including the Irish Brigade, caught the gray defenders by surprise. The Confederates had not expected a predawn attack. The charging Yankees swarmed into the Rebel trenches with a shout, smashing through the "Mule Shoe," suffering relatively few casualties. The blue onslaught could not be stopped. Hundreds of Federal troops poured over the earthworks in triumph.

Vicious hand-to-hand combat erupted between blue and gray in the dark, water-filled trenches of the "Mule Shoe" salient. The fighting was so savage in the embattled salient that many soldiers swore that it was the most nightmarish contest of the war. Waving the green flag before the attacking soldiers of the Twenty-eighth Massachusetts, Color Sgt. Peter Welsh was mortally wounded. He was struck in the left arm by a bullet and died in a Washington, D.C. hospital on May 28.

When least expected, a counterattacking Rebel division struck the victors in blue. Lee hurled other troops forward to drive the Yankees back to the muddy trenches, where they had broken through with fantasies that the war might be won on this hellish day.

The two sides remained in place and continued to fight on with stubborn tenacity. Extending far into the night with blue and gray battling each other on either side of the fortifications, the fighting at Spotsylvania continued hour after hour. The close-range combat was so vicious that this embattled sector became known as "the Bloody Angle." A member of the Sixty-ninth New York, John Noonan, wrote: "There was only a log revetment between the combatants through which they fired into each others' faces [and] men brained and bayoneted each other over the top [of the earthworks with] The rain poring [sic] down but could not chill the ardor of the combatants."

More Irish Brigade soldiers died in the mud and rain of "the Bloody Angle," reminiscent of the slaughter at "the Bloody Lane" of Antietam. There was no decisive victory; the result of the nightmarish fighting at Spotsylvania Court House was only a spiraling casualty rate for the Irish Brigade and for no gain.

Indeed, at Spotsylvania, nearly 11,000 Union soldiers fell, while Lee lost about half that number. Despite the heavy losses, Grant was more determined that ever to continue offensive operations to wear down the Army of Northern Virginia and to push ever closer to Richmond.

What Grant had unleashed was a relentless campaign calculated to wear down the manpower and fighting resolve of the Army of Northern Virginia. This formula for decisive victory, however, exacted an ever-rising toll not only counted in dead and wounded, but also in the mental make-up of the Union soldiers. Like the northern populace, the hard-fighting men of the Army of the Potomac became more fatigued and war-weary with the endless fighting for seemingly no gain.

Since Grant's men crossed the Rapidan River in the first days of May, the slaughter had been severe. The Twenty-eighth Massachusetts lost nearly 200 men in only a few weeks. Along with the ever-soaring losses of so many friends and relatives in the Celtic ranks, the continuous savage fighting was too much for even some of the best Irish Brigade soldiers.

For the relative handful of survivors from the old Irish Brigade, the horrific memories of Antietam and Fredericksburg now combined with the Wilderness fighting to linger like demons that could not be easily exorcised. This brutal combat haunted the Irish soldiers in the ranks, bringing forth nightmares. Irish Brigade officers began to wear mourning badges on the left shoulder of their blue uniform coats to honor the seemingly endless number of fallen Irish soldiers.

Despite the losses, the shattered remains of the Irish Brigade continued to engage in the aggressive offensive operations to wear down the Army of Northern Virginia. Additional fighting flared along the lines with almost constant clashes between armies. Shifting some units eastward in an attempt to out-flank the Army of Northern Virginia, Grant discovered that Lee had countered by also moving some units in the same direction to parry the new threat. These southern troop movements told the ever-vigilant Grant that the old defensive line at Spotsylvania had been weakened. Grant hoped that this altered tactical situation now presented an opportunity for his troops to smash through the same Confederate defenses, now considerably weakened, that he had assaulted in vain on May 12.

On May 18, consequently, Hancock's troops of the Second Corps struck once again at the Confederate line at Spotsylvania in the hope that it had been sufficiently weakened for an easy breakthrough. Awaiting an attack, the Southerners had constructed a sturdy second defensive line inside the "Mule Shoe" salient, and it held firm under the onslaught.

Losses among the Irish Brigade again were high. A grief-stricken Lt. Rufus P. King wrote: "Our men of the Brigade had to rush at them through a storm of grape and rifle-balls. Men dropped in scores, but the rest never faltered; and our springing into the outer ditch, the rebels, after dreadful havoc in their ranks, broke . . . but, on their being heavily reinforced, they returned and drove us out. Again we drove them from the rifle-pits, but only after terrible slaughter, in which our Brigade got very much shattered . . . ."

Finally, the determined, but futile, Union assaults were called off. The receding blue lines left behind new piles of dead and wounded comrades. The bloodied survivors of the Irish Brigade limped back to their encampment in the haunted pine forests, after losing more good men for no gain. One particular loss among the Irish was not serious, sparking Irish humor and laughter. Robert Glendenning, Company K, 116th Pennsylvania, "had his wig carried away by a passing shell, and the boys thought his head was gone, but he turned up all right, though very bald."

As demonstrated so often in the past, the Union assaults against strong defenses led in the same predictable, bloody results: many soldiers lost for no decisive result, despite some initial gains. The red clay soil in this part of Virginia was destined to receive quite a few more dead Irishmen, who would never again see their homeland of emerald green.

At the end of May, having completing his Boston recruiting mission, Col. Richard Byrnes, the former commander of the Twenty-eighth Massachusetts, took charge of the depleted Irish Brigade. Colonel Smyth left with much regret after having provided solid leadership as the Irish Brigade's commander. Colonel Byrnes was the most senior regimental commander of the Irish Brigade at this time, so Smyth received another assignment.

Overall, Byrnes was a fine officer of promise and a tough disciplinarian. From the beginning, Color Sergeant Welsh fully understood that the strong influence of the capable Colonel Byrnes was absolutely necessary to transform the Bay State Irishmen into better soldiers, because "there is one thing certain that Irishmen as a general rule are good soldiers but they must have oficers [sic] who are strict military men." From beginning to end, Byrnes, possessing more than fifteen years of experience as a United States regular, was an effective disciplinarian who got good results. He had risen in the ranks not through cutthroat politics and self-promotion, but from outstanding leadership ability and demonstrated valor on the battlefield.

Ignoring the loss of nearly 40,000 men since crossing the Rapidan River, Grant continued to advance relentlessly deeper into central Virginia, and ever-closer to Richmond. All the while, he attempted to turn Lee's flank by extending his left to overlap the right of the Army of Northern Virginia. These strategic turning movements meant that the Irish soldiers spent most of each day marching through the steaming summer weather, dusty roads, and thick woodlands of Virginia.

Both armies steadily shifted southeastward in parallel maneuvering that took them ever closer to Richmond. Lee continued to withdraw until he reached the crossroads at Cold Harbor, just northeast of Richmond and about halfway between the James and Pamunkey Rivers. Here, where five dirt roads met, the Army of Northern Virginia made a stand. The Rebels dug in for the inevitable Union assault. Ignoring all advice to retire north of the Rapidan, Grant's strategy of constant turning movements was destined to pay high dividends in the end. The Army of Northern Virginia made a final stand before Richmond, because another successful strategic movement by Grant would force Lee's troops into the defenses around Richmond and Petersburg, taking away Lee's opportunities to maneuver.

As if to further remind the Irish Brigade soldiers that the horrors of the frontal assaults at Antietam and Fredericksburg were not aberrations, Grant then committed the ultimate folly by hurling three corps at the strong defensive position held by Lee's army at Cold Harbor. This offensive effort on the early morning of June 3 was the greatest frontal assault ever undertaken by the Army of the Potomac. The Irish Brigade was not spared slaughter on this bloody day. General Grant was gambling, hoping to win it all in a desperate bid to end the war with one blow.

With Richmond less than a dozen miles away and with Lee's Army battered from a constant pounding and endless maneuvering toward Richmond, Grant believed that a good chance existed for the Army of the Potomac, despite its

Gen. Ulysses S. Grant at his headquarters at Cold Harbor, Virginia.

heavy losses since crossing the Rapidan, to break through the ever-thinning Confederate lines with a massive frontal assault. As at Spotsylvania, thousands of Rebels, with their backs to Richmond and a determination to hold firm, were waiting behind massive fortifications of red clay amid the sun-baked countryside.

In the assault, the Irish soldiers "fell in heaps," wrote diminutive Capt. James Flemming, of the Twenty-eighth Massachusetts. Leading the Irish Brigade forward in the manner of General Meagher at Antietam and Fredericksburg was Byrnes. The young colonel was at the head of his charging Celtic troops, leading by inspirational example, when he was fatally cut down a bullet through his spine.

And, as at Spotsylvania Court House, the hard-won gains in capturing the Southern earthworks at Cold Harbor were temporary. The works could not be held or exploited, thanks to a vicious crossfire and a swarm of counterattacking Rebels. Finding themselves in an exposed position, the Irish Brigade soldiers were hit by flank fires on both sides. Additional sons of Erin went down to the vicious crossfire, falling to rise no more.

With the veil of darkness of June 3, the hard-hit Yankees, including the Irish, retired under the protective cover of the night. The beaten Federals withdrew with nothing to show for their efforts, except more futile heroics that had been blasted to pieces by the merciless fire of Confederate musketry and artillery.

The Irish Brigade's strength had steadily eroded from the beginning of the Richland Campaign, diminishing like a hot summer slipping into autumn's cool.

Since the battle of the Wilderness in early May, the Irish Brigade had lost 974 men killed, wounded, and captured. Major Mulholland was wounded in three different battles in the month of May alone. A good many other top Irish Brigade officers were likewise killed or wounded during the bitter fighting.

Clearly, Grant made his greatest mistake of the campaign in deciding to assault the powerful trenches of Cold Harbor on June 3. In only around fifteen minutes, the Army of the Potomac lost nearly 7,000 men. Once again, as during the suicidal assaults on Marye's Heights at Fredericksburg, the Army of Northern Virginia had delivered a severe blow upon the Union Army, while losing only around 1,500 soldiers.

However, the deadly chess game between generals Grant and Lee was only beginning after the slaughter at Cold Harbor. Exhausted, the two armies remained in position around Cold Harbor for two weeks. In mid-June, Grant resumed the initiative vigorously and edged his army farther south and toward the James River.

After the death of Byrnes, Col. Patrick Kelly, veteran of the Sixty-ninth New York State Militia and the former commander of the Eighty-eighth New York, once again took command of the diminished Irish Brigade. By this time, the Brigade continued to be only a mere shadow of its former self. Kelly was a large man with "the physique of Hercules." This imposing physique ensured a strong command presence whenever Colonel Kelly was on the battlefield.

Petersburg, the key railroad and supply center just below the capital of Richmond, now became the principal objective of Grant's relentless campaign to end the life of the Army of

The extensive Confederate fortifications around Petersburg, Virginia.

Northern Virginia, and hence the Confederacy. Grant knew that if he could capture Petersburg, then Richmond would be doomed.

The first troops of the Army of the Potomac reached the outskirts of the Confederate defenses protecting Petersburg, before Lee and the Army of Northern Virginia could reinforce the diminutive Petersburg garrison. The initial Union attacks against the lightly-defended earthworks protecting the city came on June 15. A band of determined Southern defenders narrowly repulsed Grant's first strikes to overpower Petersburg's defenses.

On the hot afternoon of June 16, the Irish Brigade assaulted the defensive lines of Petersburg where they overran the first line of the Confederate defenses; the Yankees possessed visions of a quick victory. Then Colonel Kelly was killed when hit in the head by a bullet. As so often in the past, the Confederates rallied and stood firm against the raging blue tide, while Rebel reinforcements counterattacked to drive the Yankees from the captured earthworks. Once again, Union assaults launched against a fortified position were in vain, resulting in high casualties. More Irish Brigade soldiers were killed or maimed for no immediate strategic gain, a tragic pattern that steadily sapped the manpower and of the brigade.

The defenders of the Confederacy's last citadel had stood firm. Now Grant was forced to reduce Petersburg with a lengthy siege, eventually lasting for ten months, the longest siege of the Civil War. General Grant's ambitious plan for achieving a quick decisive victory evaporated like the future plans of the many Irish Brigade soldiers who were no more.

The loss of Colonel Kelly was a devastating blow for the Irish Brigade. He was an inspirational example for the Irish soldiers, both on and off the battlefield. In an army command structure where giant egos and political maneuvering dominated the officer ranks, the good-natured Kelly was modest and unassuming. Hence, the capable Irishman was greatly respected by one and all. One Eighty-eighth New York soldier never forgot the sad burial of their beloved colonel, writing in a sad letter: "Over his lifeless body, on its being brought from under fire, by order of Capt. Maurice W. Wall, commanding the 69th New York . . . strong old veteran soldiers wept like children and wrung their hands in frenzy."

From June 15 to June 30, the Irish Brigade lost another 248 men in fighting that seemed to have no end. After Colonel Kelly's death, Capt. Richard Moroney, Sixty-ninth New York, assumed command of what little remained of the Irish Brigade. The majority of the Irish field officers who had begun the spring campaign and crossed the Rapidan River with optimistic visions of a swift capture of Richmond were either killed or wounded. The high attrition rate ensured not only the further erosion but also the fragmentation of the Irish Brigade. During this period, the depleted Twenty-eighth Massachusetts was transferred out of the Irish Brigade. Then, the 116th Pennsylvania, battered and with its ranks thinned like those of the Twenty-eighth Massachusetts, was assigned to another brigade.

In late June 1864, one Irish soldier lamented the thorough dissolution of the Irish Brigade, writing "it is a Brigade no longer and without the protection of Providence, the remnant of our heroic little Brigade will lose what it has won; for all that now remains of it is the recollection of its service and sufferings."

In fact, all that remained of the once mighty Irish Brigade was its three small New York regiments. These three remaining regiments from New York City now became part of a "Consolidated Brigade," with other units. At least officially and on paper, the Irish Brigade was no more, as General Meagher had feared in 1862.

The fighting continued unabated during the siege of Petersburg, as General Grant sought to destroy the railroad lines supplying food and munitions to Petersburg and Lee's Army. Several engagements were fought around Petersburg with the Irishmen serving as members of this "Consolidated Brigade." The largest of these actions erupted on August 25, 1864, when more Irish soldiers died during the fighting at Reams' Station, when Grant pushed the Second Corps forward to cut the rail lines of the Weldon Railroad supplying Petersburg. The Confederates captured 85 Celtic warriors during the contest at Reams' Station. This total included excellent soldiers like Capt. Maurice W. Wall, Sixty-ninth New York. Captain Wall cursed his unlucky fate to fall "into the hands of the Philistines." A native of County Tipperary, Ireland, Captain Wall, "reliable, and intelligent," had served in Meagher's Company K of the old Sixty-ninth New York State Militia.

The brutal slugfest between the Army of the Potomac and the Army of Northern Virginia continued throughout the summer of 1864. The constant fighting led to the virtual extinction of the remaining fragments of the Irish Brigade. Gloom settled over the little band of Celtic survivors, who had seen far too many friends and relatives slaughtered for no gain during a lengthy series of battles that seemed to have no decisive result or end. One Irish Brigade soldier, who was one of the few lucky ones to have survived the butchery, lamented with a mixture of horror and sadness how this command of Irish warriors simply "was a Brigade no longer."

Richard Moroney, now promoted major, continued in command of what little was left of the Irish Brigade He was a veteran of the old Sixty-ninth New York State Militia at a time when it seemed as if the war could be won in only a few weeks. After recovering from a wound received in the Wheat Field of Gettysburg, the Petersburg campaign found Major Moroney ready for action and a significant leadership role. But Moroney's command was very temporary.

With the summer of 1864, the Celtic regiments of the once proud Irish Brigade were dispersed and reassigned to other brigades of the Second Corps to bolster the strength of other Union brigades throughout the corps. The Irish Brigade was officially abolished because of the attrition that had culled its ranks unmercifully. As a disillusioned Cpl. Samuel Clear, 116th Pennsylvania, penned in a letter: "The old Irish Brigade is a thing of the past. There never was a better one [that] pulled their triggers on the Johnnies."

But like the legendary phoenix rising from the ashes in mystical fashion, so the Irish Brigade would also be resurrected when least expected. Mounting anger and protests from the Irish community of New York City applied pressure on the War Department for the reconstitution of the Irish Brigade. Energetic officers busily sought to gain as many recruits as possible in order to "start the Brigade again." The three New York regiments were removed from the "Consolidated Brigade" and the Twenty-eighth Massachusetts was ordered back to join the new, or the second, Irish Brigade. The rejuvenated Irish Brigade even gained a new unit to bolster its strength, the Seventh New York Heavy Artillery.

On the third anniversary of the historic founding of the Irish Brigade on September 4, 1864, a festive celebration was held in honor of the resurrected Irish Brigade. Meagher and Fathers Corby and Ouellet played prominent roles on this memorable occasion. The mounting pressure from the home front and from the Irish Brigade survivors had brought about a successful effort to restore the old Irish Brigade once again.

After the reactivation of the Irish Brigade in November 1864, the morale of the Irish soldiers soared to new heights. The reforming of the Irish Brigade by the War Department was largely a bureaucratic exercise in paperwork. After the former regiments of the Irish Brigade had joined together once again, the return of many wounded veterans and additional recruitment bolstered the thinned ranks.

Col. Robert Nugent became the last commander in the Irish Brigade's history. He was a former member of the United States regulars and second in command of the Sixty-ninth New York State Militia at the battle of First Bull Run, in addition to being a good friend of General Meagher. Nugent survived a nasty wound at Fredericksburg. By any measure, Colonel Nugent was a proven and highly respected leader.

The new Irish Brigade continued to fight on with the Army of the Potomac, which was getting closer to decisive victory with each passing day. The Irishmen engaged in a number of battles and skirmishes throughout the siege of Petersburg. One highlight in the monotonous siege warfare was the feat performed by Capt. Murtha Murphy, a native of County Wexford in southeast Ireland. He single-handedly captured an entire company of thirteen Rebels, including their commanding officer.

By early February 1865 during the siege of Petersburg, the Irish Brigade was composed of around 1,600 soldiers.

But these seemingly high numbers were misleading, because the men in the ranks at this time little resembled the hardened veterans of late 1862. After the customary High Mass, the brigade's final festive celebration of St. Patrick's Day was held on March 17, 1865. Besides other amusements, a plentiful flow of alcohol helped to ease the haunting memory of so many lost comrades and the surreal horrors of this war, which was becoming increasingly more brutal. Only a relative handful of veteran officers and men survived to remember the glory days of the Irish Brigade. Indeed, the Sixtyninth New York suffered the sixth highest losses in killed and wounded of all the Union regiments in the Civil War, while the Twenty-eighth Massachusetts ranked seventh.

However, Irish Brigade's spirit lived on and would never fade away. This reality ensured that the Celtic unit would play yet another active role in the last campaign of the war, the Appomattox Campaign. As throughout the conflict, the emerald green banners of the Irish Brigade continued to inspire the men in the ranks to do the impossible. As Capt. David Conyngham explained with some emotion: "This green flag, with its ancient harp, its burst of sunlight, and it motto from Ossian, in the old Irish tongue, recalls through the long lapse of many centuries the period when Ireland was a nation. . . ."

Throughout the winter of 1865, the Army of the Potomac gathered strength for the final campaign of the war. It was now only a matter of time before the besieged Confederates of a ever-dwindling army and a dying city and nation would be forced to evacuate Petersburg. In the spring of 1865, Grant prepared to deliver a death blow to the Army of Northern Virginia and the beleaguered Confederacy.

Lee and his top commanders realized that time was not on their side. Instead of waiting for the inevitable defeat, Lee decided to make one last attempt to break through the blue ring of Grant's besieging troops. He launched a massive attack on Fort Stedman. Located east of Petersburg, Fort Stedman was a strong point that anchored the center of the sprawling Union defensive line.

The idea to attack Fort Stedman to break the siege of Petersburg, defeat General Grant's Army, and perhaps reverse the course of the war came from the fertile mind of Gen. James B. Gordon, now one of Lee's best corps commanders. He was a regimental commander in the brigade of Alabama troops, who had slaughtered so many Irish soldiers at "the Bloody Lane" at Antietam. The Confederate assault, containing nearly half the strength of General Lee's army, struck Fort Stedman in the early morning hours of March 25. The Rebel onslaught initially achieved considerable gains, but the counterattacking Yankees eventually restored the line and recaptured the fort. As on so many past battlefields, the Irish Brigade troops played a key role in repulsing the Confederate breakthrough.

Employing his favorite tactic once again, General Grant shifted his troops below Petersburg to outflank the Army of Northern Virginia on the right, and then launched a series of hard-hitting attacks. This maneuvering resulted in the cutting of the railroad line west of the city, forcing Petersburg's evacuation in early April. Not only was Petersburg now doomed, but also Richmond. Lee and his army now had only one hope for survival: escape Virginia and the Army of the Potomac to conduct a long march south to reach northern

Fort Stedman near Petersburg, Virginia.

North Carolina and link with the army of Gen. Joseph E. Johnston.

By early April and less than two weeks after celebrating the final St. Patrick's Day in the history of the Irish Brigade, Nugent's troops joined in the vigorous westward pursuit of Lee's ragged army. A rejuvenated Army of the Potomac closed in on its wounded opponent in an attempt to apply the final death stroke. It was now a race between Grant's army and the Army of Northern Virginia westward through the springtime forests of the Appomattox River country.

On April 2, the fast-pursuing Irish soldiers smashed through Lee's rear-guard. Without hesitating or celebrating the success, the Irish Yankees continued onward, sensing the kill. The attackers in blue, however, ran into a strong defensive line consisting of two Confederate redoubts connected by a long defensive line of trenches. Demonstrating more typical Irish fighting spirit, the cheering Celtic soldiers tore though a abatis of felled trees and surged ahead, but fell back when hit by a blistering fire.

After regrouping and in conjunction with other Union troops, the attacking Irish captured the strong redoubt with a cheer. Out-pacing other Yankee units, the men of the "fighting Sixty-ninth" were the first bluecoats to swarm into the redoubt. Without pausing, the Irishmen then continued onward to overwhelm the next redoubt. After yet another charge the Irish soldiers captured scores of Confederate prisoners, artillery pieces, and even a Rebel battle-flag on April 2.

Four days later on April 6, Col. Robert Nugent led the Irish Brigade through the wet farmlands toward Amelia Court House, west of Petersburg and on the south side of the Appomattox River. Leading the way on his favorite charger, "Harry," Nugent ordered his men forward to smash into the Confederate rear-guard once again. As before, the weary Rebels fell back, and the Irish soldiers pursued their beaten opponents for miles. Exploiting their success, the Celtic soldiers overran a Confederate wagon train and captured additional prisoners, as more Army of Northern Virginia units disintegrated with each passing mile.

Despite the terrible attrition rate that had left the Irish Brigade a mere shadow of its former self, enough good men remained in the ranks to fully appreciate the meaning of a final skirmish outside the small village of Farmville, Virginia, southwest of Richmond and east of Appomattox Court House, on April 7, 1865. Near this small town, a former commander of the Irish Brigade, Gen. Thomas A. Smyth, was killed. Two days later, on a Palm Sunday that the Irish Brigade troops would never forget, General Lee surrendered the battered remains of his depleted army at Appomattox Court House.

Colonel Nugent wrote of the last day of active campaigning for the Irish Brigade: "resumed the march at 7 a.m., and moved about six miles where we await action of conference between the respective commanders" of two armies that had been slaughtering each other for years, and until this decisive moment.

Nugent had come full circle: having served as a United States regular and then as the lieutenant colonel of the "Fighting Sixty-ninth" at First Bull Run, where he had witnessed the first major Union defeat of the war. And now nearly four years later, Nugent was commanding a brigade of Irishmen in a formidable Union army that had finally achieved decisive victory over Lee and his battered command. The grueling Appomattox campaign against a desperate opponent cost the Irish Brigade another 100 soldiers. Gen. Robert E. Lee's surrender led to the collapse of the Confederate war effort on both sides of the Mississippi.

The staggering loss of more than 4,000 Irish soldiers was the inevitable price for establishing a nation-wide reputation as the elite combat unit of the Army of the Potomac. Few brigades on either side lost as many men in combat as the Irish Brigade, and none in more key battlefield situations during some of the war's greatest engagements.

The percentage of Irishmen in "Meagher's Brigade" killed or mortally wounded on the battlefield was staggering. The Sixty-ninth New York lost the most men, with a total of 259 killed or mortally wounded soldiers in the war. This was closely followed by the Twenty-eighth Massachusetts, which had 250 soldiers killed or mortally wounded. Both these units ranked in the top ten of more than 2,000 Federal regiments in regard to the highest fatalities of all Union regiments which served during the four years of war.

And in regard to the number of fatalities in the Irish Brigade, the Sixty-third New York ranked third, with 156 killed or mortally wounded. This was followed by the Eighty-eighth New York, which lost 151 in killed and mortally wounded. The 116th Pennsylvania suffered a total loss of 145 either killed or wounded.

Unlike the majority of brigades of both sides in the Civil War, the Irish Brigade never lost a battle-flag. Conyngham and other Irish soldiers were especially proud that "no flag of the Irish Brigade has ever yet emblazoned a rebel display, though they captured more than twenty of the enemy's colors."

Even long after Lee's surrender at Appomattox, the war was still not yet over for many Irish Brigade soldiers.

Moroney returned home after the war's end, but found neither peace nor prosperity. The major, a veteran of the Mexican-American War, never completely recovered from his bad Gettysburg wound and the ravages of disease. He died on December 29, 1865, more than six months after Lee's surrender. Other Irish Brigade veterans continued to die of both disease and battle wounds long after the guns of the Civil War had ceased firing in anger.

Epilogue

In the annals of Civil War historiography, the distinguished legacy of the Irish Brigade is that of one of the elite combat units and best fighting commands on either side from 1861-1865. But the true importance of the Irish Brigade transcended its superior combat performances during some of the most decisive and hardest fought battles of the Civil War.

Indeed, in many ways, the most important legacy of the Irish Brigade can be understood in terms of what really motivated and inspired these young Irish immigrants and second generation Irishmen. These soldiers from far-away Ireland and from the Irish ghettoes and lower middle class Celtic communities of Boston, New York City, Philadelphia and other cities and rural communities across the North fought and died at such hellish places as Antietam, Fredericksburg, and Gettysburg for the fulfillment of the golden dream of America, especially its promises of religious, political, and social freedoms, and personal liberties for all men as promised by the Declaration of Independence.

Perhaps Color Sgt. Peter Welsh, the devout Catholic warrior and flag-bearer of the Twenty-eighth Massachusetts, best perceived the true meaning of the Irish Brigade and how the many Irishmen who fell had not died in vain, because the dream of America has continued to endure for millions of new immigrants from lands around the world. As he said in a letter to his wife Margaret:

> Seven centuries of persecution [with Catholic] Churches[,] Convents [,] and Monesteries [*sic*] plundered and destroyed [along with a legacy of] Conviscated [*sic*] property [and] Murdered [Irish] patriots and innocent women and children slaughtered in cold blood [and] With inumerable [*sic*] other barbarities of the most fiendish discription [*sic*] which from time to time have been comited [*sic*] in unfortunate Irland [*sic*] by that prostitute of [all] nations . . . called the British Government . . . In this country it is very different [as] Here we have a free government [with] just laws and a Constitution which guarantees equal rights and privelages [*sic*] for all[.] Here thousands of the sons and daughters of Irland [*sic*] have come to seek a refuge from tyrany [*sic*] and persecution at home[.] And thousands still continue to come[.] Here they have an open field for industry[.] And those who posses the abilitys [*sic*] can raise themselves to positions of honor and emolument. Here Irishmen and their decendents [*sic*] have a claim [in] a stake in the nation and an interest in its prosperity . . . America is Irlands [*sic*] refuge [and] Irlands [*sic*] best hope [and] destroy this republic and her hopes [and those of the rest of the world] are blasted.

Here, in simple but eloquent words, Color Sergeant Welsh articulated the fundamental reason why the soldiers of the Irish Brigade fought so hard and well: for egalitarian principles and the salvation and the future of the Irish people on both sides of the Atlantic.

Capt. David Power Conyngham, who served on Meagher's staff, agreed with the idealistic color sergeant who sacrificed his life for his beliefs. "The Irish felt that not only was the safety of the great [American] Republic, the home of their exiled race, at stake, but also, that the great principles of democracy were at issue with the aristocratic doctrines of monarchism [and] Should the latter prevail, there was no longer any hope for the struggling nationalists of the Old World."

In addition, another important motivation of the Irish Brigade soldiers was to gain the experience in preparation for the future attempt to fulfill the golden dream of liberating Ireland from British rule. But that burning ambition had died on the battlefields of Virginia, Maryland, and Pennsylvania during the brutal fighting of the Seven Days, before the Sunken Road of Antietam, at the stone wall before Marye's Heights, in the Wheat Field of Gettysburg, in the bloody Richmond Campaign, and in the struggle to gain possession of Petersburg. It died with the thousands of the best and brightest sons of Erin from both sides of the Atlantic, who gave their lives in those terrible battles.

In the words of one Irish Brigade soldier, who survived the holocaust: "On the bloody fields of Virginia . . . lie the bleached bones of many an Irish soldier," who had fought and died in a strange land. Like the desire to see family one final time, the future dream of Ireland's liberation died with them thousands of miles away from their homeland on the other side of the Atlantic. Those young Irish soldiers, who were to have gained the necessary combat and leadership experience in the Civil War to have been utilized in liberating the Green Isle from British rule now filled individual graves and crowded burial trenches across Virginia, Maryland, and Pennsylvania.

In a final tragic lament, Meagher described the bitter end for so many young Irish soldiers: "All of them were from Ireland, and as the tide of life rushed out, the last thought that left their hearts was for the liberty of Ireland."

During the grand victory parade of the Army of the Potomac down Washington's Pennsylvania Avenue on a hot May 22, 1865, Nugent led the few survivors of the Irish Brigade with well-justified pride. These Celtic veterans now wore green sprigs of boxwood in their hats in honor of old Ireland, the Irish Brigade's suicidal charge at Fredericksburg, and the hundreds of comrades who were no more.

The last appearance of the Irish Brigade came in early July 1865, when the handful of surviving Irish soldiers returned to New York City. As reported in the July 4, 1865, issue of the *New York Times*: "The famous and now long-tried Irish Brigade, under the command of Brevet Brig. Gen. Robert Nugent, arrived early yesterday morning . . . The brigade has an extensive and gallant record, having shared in the glory of every engagement fought by the army of the Potomac, since its organization . . . ." The next day, July 5, 1865, the Irish Brigade marched one last time through the streets of New

York City, demonstrating its discipline and pride before the Irish people of New York City and a cheering throng.

Once again in this final act, the distinctive Irish pride, esprit de corps, and spirit of the Irish Brigade soldiers had risen to the fore, as on so many past battlefields. The sterling performance of these Irishmen on battlefields from 1862-1865 had accomplished much to negate the anti-Irish, anti-Catholic, and anti-immigrant feeling that was so prevalent across America. In this sense and in the end, the Irish Brigade soldiers were successful in winning their personal war on two fronts: an enduring legacy for the American nation and the Irish people.

In far-away Ireland, the legacy of the brilliant combat performances and high sacrifices of the Irish Brigade was quickly forgotten. Only the relatives of the many Irish soldiers who had fallen on distant battlefields of America remembered those sons, brothers, and fathers, and cousins, who had died on the other side of the Atlantic at places with strange-sounding names that they had never heard before and would never see.

But the Irish family of Capt. Patrick Clooney felt the need to leave behind a lasting tribute to their twenty-two-year-old son, who was killed at Antietam. The first enduring memorial to an Irish Brigade soldier on the Green Isle was dedicated on February 21, 1863, from funds donated by the people of Waterford in a community response to the loss of one of its most promising sons. In his old neighborhood of Ballybricken, a suburb of Waterford, a stone obelisk was erected in Captain Clooney's memory in the Ballybricken Churchyard behind the stone church, where his Catholic family had worshiped for generations.

Carefully cut and carved by a master stone mason, the words on the memorial highlighted Captain Clooney's military service, as a member of the famed St. Patrick's Battalion in Italy, and as an officer of the Irish Brigade in America. While Captain Clooney's body lay in a shallow grave in the rich, dark soil of Washington County, Maryland, so far away, the Clooney family in Waterford felt the solace of a permanent memorial to their son and a constant reminder that made them feel like young Patrick was finally at home in the "old sod" of Ireland to rest eternally in peace.

In the end, all that remained of the Irish Brigade, besides the hundreds of Irishmen lying in graves across the haunted fields, swamps, and thickets of Virginia, Maryland, and Pennsylvania, was the ghostly memory, in the words of Capt. David Power Conyngham, of the high-spirited "Irish cheer, such as never before shook the woods of old Virginia, swelling and rolling far and wide into the gleaming air."

Indeed, the Irish Brigade's distinctive Gaelic war-cry of "Faugh-a-Ballaugh" was now only a distant, haunting memory, and little more than a fading reminder of a fraternity of what had been a band of idealistic young Irish soldiers, who fought and died far-away from their native Celtic homeland and families to fulfill the dream of America for themselves and future generations of Irish. This was the real, enduring legacy left behind by General Meagher and the hard-fighting Celtic soldiers of the Irish Brigade.

Bibliography

Asbury, Herbert. *The Gangs of New York* (New York: Thunder's Mouth Press, 1998).

Bartlett, Thomas and Jeffrey, Keith. *A Military History of Ireland* (Cambridge, N.Y.: Cambridge University Press, 1996).

Bilby, Joseph G. *Remember Fontenoy! The 69th New York and the Irish Brigade in the Civil War.* (Hightstown, N.J.: Longstreet House, 1995).

Bilby, Joseph G., and O'Neill, Stephen D. *"My Sons Were Faithful and They Fought," The Irish Brigade at Antietam, An Anthology.* (Hightstown, N.J.: Longstreet House, 1997).

Bowden, Scott and Ward, Bill. *Last Chance For Victory, Robert E. Lee and the Gettysburg Campaign.* (New York: Da Capo Press, 2001).

Brooks, Thomas Walter, and Jones, Michael Dan. *Lee's Foreign Legion, A History of the 10th Louisiana Infantry.* (Gravenhurst, Canada: Watts Printing, 1995).

Compiled Service Records of Union Troops Who Served in Organizations from the States of New York, Massachusetts, and Pennsylvania. National Archives. Washington, D.C.

Conyngham, David Power. *The Irish Brigade.* Introduction by Lawrence Frederick Kohl. (New York: Fordham University Press, 1994).

Cronin, Sean. *For Whom the Hangman's Noose was Spun, Wolfe Tone and the United Irishmen.* (Dublin: Repsol Publishing, 1991).

Cullen, Joseph P. *The Peninsula Campaign 1862.* (New York: Bonanza Books, n.d.)

Cusack, Mary Frances. *An Illustrated History of Ireland, From AD 400 to 1800.* (London: Bracken Books, 1995).

Doyle, Danny and Terrence Folan. *The Gold Sun of Irish Freedom, 1798 in Song and Story.* (Dublin: Mercier Press, 1998).

Eagleton, Terry. *Scholars and Rebels in Nineteenth-Century Ireland.* (Malden, Mass.: Blackwell Publishers, Ltd., 1999).

Foster, R.F., ed. *The Oxford History of Ireland.* (Oxford: Oxford University Press, 1992).

Golway, Terry. *For the Cause of Liberty, A Thousand Years of Ireland's Heroes.* (New York: Simon and Schuster, 2000).

Gordon, John B. *Reminiscences of the Civil War.* (New York: Scribner's Sons, 1904).

The Irish American. New York City.

Irish Brigade Collection, Fredericksburg and Spotsylvania National Military Park. Fredericksburg, Virginia.

Kee, Robert. *The Green Flag, A History of Irish Nationalism.* (New York: Penguin Books, 2000).

Keneally, Thomas. *The Great Shame, and the Triumph of the Irish in the English-Speaking World.* (New York: Anchor Books, 1998).

Kenny, Michael. *The 1798 Rebellion.* (Dublin: Town House and Country House, 1996).

Kohl, Lawrence Frederick and Margaret Cosse Richard, eds. *Irish Green and Union Blue: The Civil War Letters of Peter Welsh.* (New York: Fordham University Press, 1986).

Landis, Allen, Letters. Manuscript Division. Library of Congress. Washington, D.C.

Leyburn, James G. *The Scotch-Irish, A Social History.* (Chapel Hill: University of North Carolina Press, 1962).

Litton, Helen. *Irish Rebellions, 1798-1916,* (Niwot, Co.: The Irish American Book Company, 1998).

MacManus, Seumas. *The Story of the Irish Race.* (New York: The Devin-Adair Company, 1969).

McDonald, JoAnna M., ed. *The Faces of Irish Civil War Soldiers.* (Redondo Beach, Calif.: Rank and File Publications, 1999).

McPherson, James M. *Battle Cry of Freedom: The Civil War Era.* (Oxford: Oxford University Press, 1988).

McWhiney, Grady, and Perry D. Jamieson. *Attack and Die: Civil War Military Tactics and the Southern Heritage.* (Tuscaloosa: University of Alabama Press, 1990).

Mulholland, St. Clair A. *The Story of a Regiment.* (Gaithersburg, Md.: Old Soldier Books, Inc., n.d.).

The Munster Express. Waterford, Ireland.

Murphy, T.L. *Kelly's Heroes: The Irish Brigade at Gettysburg.* (Gettysburg: Farnsworth House Military Impressions, 1997).

The New York Herald. New York, New York.

The *New York Times.* New York, New York.

O'Brien, Kevin E. *My Life in the Irish Brigade: The Civil War Memoirs of Private William McCarter, 116th Pennsylvania Infantry.* (Campbell, Calif.: Savas Publishing Company, 1996).

O'Donnell, Ruan. *Remember Emmet: Images of the Life and Legacy of Robert Emmet.* (Bray, Ireland: Wordwell Publishing, 2003).

Pakenham, Thomas. *The Year of Liberty: The Great Irish Rebellion.* (London: Weidenfeld and Nicolson, 1997).

The Pilot. Boston, Massachusetts.

Priest, John M. *Antietam: The Soldiers' Battle.* (Shippensburg, Penn.: White Mane Publishing Company, 1989).

Pritchard, Russ A., Jr. *The Irish Brigade: A Pictorial History of the Famed Civil War Fighters* (Philadelphia: Courage Books, 2004).

Regimental Files of the Sixty-ninth New York, Sixty-third New York, Eighty-eighth New York, Twenty-ninth Massachusetts. Antietam National Battlefield Military Park. Sharpsburg, Maryland.

The Riches of Clair Exhibition, Clare Museum, County Clare, Ireland.

Sears, Stephen. *Gettysburg.* (Boston: Houghton Mifflin Company, 2003).

_____. *To the Gates of Richmond: The Peninsula Campaign.* (New York: Ticknor & Fields, 1992).

_____. *Landscape Turned Red: The Battle of Antietam.* (New York: Warner Books, 1985).

Smith, William A., Letters. Lewis Leigh Collection. The United States Army Military History Institute. Carlisle Barracks. Carlisle, Pennsylvania.

Stevens, Peter F. *The Rogue's March: John Riley and the St. Patrick's Battalion, 1846-48.* (Dulles, Va.: Brassey's 1999).

Stewart, A.T.Q. *The Summer Soldiers: The 1798 Rebellion in Antrim and Down.* (Belfast: The Blackstaff Press, 1995).

Trudeau, Noah Andre. *Gettysburg: A Testing of Courage.* (New York: Harper Collins Publishers, 2002).

Tucker, Phillip Thomas. *Father John B. Bannon: The Confederacy's Fighting Chaplain.* (Tuscaloosa: University of Alabama Press, 1992).

_____, ed. *The History of the Irish Brigade.* (Fredericksburg, Va.: Sergeant Kirkland's Museum and Historical Society, Inc., 1995).

War of the Rebellion: A Compilation of Official Records of the Union and Confederate Armies. (Washington: Government Printing Office, 1880-1901).

Waterford, Ireland, History Files. Waterford City Library. Waterford, Ireland.

Welsh, Peter, Letters. The New York Historical Society. New York, New York.

Woodham-Smith, Cecil. *The Great Hunger* (New York: Harper and Row Publishers, 1962).

Wright, Steven J. *The Irish Brigade.* (Springfield, Penn.: Steven Wright Publishing, 1992).

Index

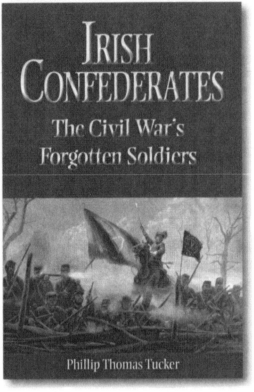